Hoodoo and Voodoo

Secrets of Folk Magic, Rootwork, Witchcraft, Mojo, Conjuration, Haitian Vodou and New Orleans Voodoo

© Copyright 2021

The contents of this book may not be reproduced, duplicated or transmitted without direct written permission from the author.

Under no circumstances will any legal responsibility or blame be held against the publisher for any reparation, damages, or monetary loss due to the information herein, either directly or indirectly.

Legal Notice:

This book is copyright protected. This is only for personal use. You cannot amend, distribute, sell, use, quote or paraphrase any part or the content within this book without the consent of the author.

Disclaimer Notice:

Please note the information contained within this document is for educational and entertainment purposes only. Every attempt has been made to provide accurate, up to date and reliable complete information. No warranties of any kind are expressed or implied. Readers acknowledge that the author is not engaging in the rendering of legal, financial, medical or professional advice. The content of this book has been derived from various sources. Please consult a licensed professional before attempting any techniques outlined in this book.

By reading this document, the reader agrees that under no circumstances is the author responsible for any losses, direct or indirect, which are incurred as a result of the use of the information contained within this document, including, but not limited to, errors, omissions, or inaccuracies.

Your Free Gift (only available for a limited time)

Thanks for getting this book! If you want to learn more about various spirituality topics, then join Mari Silva's community and get a free guided meditation MP3 for awakening your third eye. This guided meditation mp3 is designed to open and strengthen ones third eye so you can experience a higher state of consciousness. Simply visit the link below the image to get started.

https://spiritualityspot.com/meditation

Contents

PART 1: HOODOO 1
INTRODUCTION 2
CHAPTER 1: A HISTORY OF HOODOO 4
   WHAT IS VOODOO? 5
   HOODOOS CONJURE DOCTORS AND SPIRITUAL MOTHERS
   THROUGH THE AGES 7
   WHAT ROLE DOES HOODOO PLAY IN MODERN SOCIETY? 10
CHAPTER 2: HOODOO BELIEFS AND COSMOLOGY 12
   WHAT IS THE SPIRITUAL MEANING OF STARS? 16
   THE MORNING AND THE EVENING STARS 18
CHAPTER 3: THE HOODOO TOOLKIT: INGREDIENTS AND
MATERIALS 21
   WHAT IS GOOFER DUST? 21
   PLANTS AND HERBS OF HOODOO 23
   HOODOO TOOLS 26
   CROSSING PRODUCTS 28
   OTHER TOOLS THAT ARE PART OF HOODOO LORE 29
CHAPTER 4: SPIRITUAL CLEANSING BASICS 33
   PERSONAL CLEANSING 34
   QUICK-FIX METHODS OF CLEANSING YOURSELF 35
   CLEANSING AND BLESSING THE HOME 36

Cleansing Spells for Toxicity 39
CHAPTER 5: CREATING A MOJO BAG 42
CHAPTER 6: BEGIN YOUR CONJURE WORK 50
　　What is Conjure Work? 50
　　When Should You Perform Your Conjuring? 51
　　The Power of Powders 53
　　Oils 57
　　Other Types of Conjuring 58
　　Wasps Nest Conjuring 60
　　How to Enhance Your Conjure Work with Psalm
　　Recitations 60
CHAPTER 7: CANDLE MAGIC 63
　　The Meaning of Color in Hoodoo Candle Magic 64
　　Color of Candles and Their Meanings 65
　　Hoodoo Candle Terminology 66
　　Hoodoo Figure Candles 67
　　How to Read Candle Burning 69
　　Candle Flames and What They Mean 70
　　How to Read the Wax When Your Candle is Burning 71
　　How to Read the Wax Puddles Once the Candle Has Burned 72
CHAPTER 8: THE CRAFT OF ROOTWORK 73
　　Other Popular Roots and Herbs Used in Hoodoo and Their
　　Magical Properties 74
　　How to Create Amulets and Talismans with Your Roots and
　　Herbs 78
　　How to Make an Amulet 78
　　How to Make a Talisman 79
　　How to Use Magic Herbs and Roots in Your Spell Work 81
　　How to Prepare and Harvest Your Roots 81
　　Cleaning Your Roots 82
CHAPTER 9: THE HOODOO DIVINATION 83
　　Cartomancy 84
　　Card Spreads 84
　　The Definition and Meanings Behind the Cards 85

- The Individual Cards and Their Meaning 85
- How to Shuffle the Deck 88
- Augury 89
- What Different Types of Birds Mean 89
- How Many Birds Are There? 91
- How Are the Birds Behaving? 91
- How to Read Birds Flight Patterns 91
- Cleromancy 92
- How to Cure Bones 92
- How to Use Your Bones 93
- Oneiromancy 94

CHAPTER 10: HOODOO SPELLS FOR LOVE AND ATTRACTION 96
- How to Cast Spells for You and Your Partner 97
- Passion and Lust Spells 102

CHAPTER 11: HOODOO SPELLS FOR LUCK AND WEALTH 105
- Set Up An Altar Designed to Attract Luck and Wealth 106
- How to Attract Wealth and Prosperity Using Hoodoo 108

CHAPTER 12: DAILY HOODOO ROUTINES 116
- Ways to Bring Hoodoo Into Your Daily Routine 117
- How to Make Hoodoo Waters 118
- Food and Drink Related to Hoodoo 120

CONCLUSION 127

PART 2: VOODOO 128

INTRODUCTION 129

CHAPTER 1: THE VOODOO TWINS - HAITI AND NEW ORLEANS 131
- How Voodoo Started 132
- African Voodoo 133
- Introduction to Voodoo's Most Important Branches 134
- The Haitian Vodou 134
- Common Beliefs in Haitian Vodou 136
- Other Famous Beliefs 137
- Common Practices 137

    THE LOUISIANA (NEW ORLEANS VOODOO) 141
    HOW DID IT START? 141
    NEW ORLEANS (LOUISIANA VOODOO) MAJOR BELIEFS 142
    FAMOUS CHARACTERS IN NEW ORLEANS VOODOO 144
    THE MODERN NEW ORLEANS VOODOO 145

CHAPTER 2: BONDYE AND THE VOODOO GODS 147
    BONDYE IS THE SUPREME BEING 148
    VOODOO AND THE LWAS 149
    VENERATING OR WORSHIPPING THE LWA 150
    THE THREE MAIN FAMILIES OF LWA 152
    RADA LWA SPIRITS 152
    PETRO LWA SPIRITS 156
    GHEDE LWA SPIRITS 158
    THE MYSTIC MARRIAGE (MARYAJ MISTIK) 160

CHAPTER 3: BECOMING A VODOUISANT 161
    THE TRUTH ABOUT VOODOO 161
    THE BIRTH OF MISCONCEPTIONS 162
    VOODOO BELIEFS AND CHRISTIANITY 162
    RITUALS AND PRACTICES 164
    THE SOUL 165
    THE PRIESTS (HOUNGAN) AND PRIESTESSES (MAMBO) 166
    THE VOODOO TEMPLES (HOUNFO) 168
    THE INITIATION RITUALS 170
    SHOULD YOU BECOME AN INITIATE? 172

CHAPTER 4: VOODOO VEVES 174
    A CLOSER LOOK AT VEVES 174
    MOST IMPORTANT VEVES IN THE VOODOO COMMUNITY 176
    HOW TO DRAW VOODOO SYMBOLS (VEVES) 187
    USING VEVES IN TALISMANS OR FLAGS 188
    SHOULD YOU USE VEVE TATTOOS? 190

CHAPTER 5: BUILD YOUR VOODOO SHRINE 192
    TYPES OF ALTARS 192
    FINDING THE APPROPRIATE SPACE 194
    WHAT DO YOU NEED FOR YOUR VOODOO ALTAR/SHRINE? 195

    Building Your Altar 198
CHAPTER 6: HOW TO MAKE A GRIS-GRIS BAG 201
    Gris-Gris Bag Defined 202
    Ingredients for Your Gris-Gris Bag 203
    Plants and Herbs 203
    Stones and Minerals 204
    Other Materials and Objects 205
    The Actual Making of the Gris-Gris Bag 206
    Can You Make Gris-Gris Dolls? 209
CHAPTER 7: WORKING WITH DOLLS 210
    What Are Voodoo Dolls? 210
    Ideal Materials for Your Voodoo Doll 212
    Steps in Making Voodoo Dolls 214
    How to Use the Voodoo Doll 217
CHAPTER 8: THE VOODOO WAY OF LIFE 219
    Serving the Lwas 221
    Worshipping Nature and the Ancestors 221
    Daily Devotionals 222
    Voodoo vs. Christian Traditions 224
CHAPTER 9: INVOCATION AND SUMMONING RITUAL 226
    Importance of Purpose and Intention 227
    How to Invoke or Summon the Right Lwa 228
    Basic Invocation Ritual 232
    Invoking Papa Legba 233
    Some Warnings to Keep in Mind 235
CHAPTER 10: VOODOO CLEANSING AND PROTECTION SPELLS 236
    Voodoo Cleansing Spells for Your Home 236
    Using Candles for Cleansing 239
    Using Sea Salt for Cleansing 239
    Using Incense for Cleansing 240
    How to Cleanse Your Body 241
    Cleansing Water Spell 242
    Voodoo Spell of Protection 242

How to Break a Curse or Hex 243
CHAPTER 11: VOODOO LOVE SPELLS 246
　　Voodoo Spell to Make Someone Fall in Love 246
　　Voodoo Spell to Bring Back Your Ex 248
　　Voodoo Break-Up Spell 249
　　Attract Love With a Gris-Gris Bag 251
　　A Warning When Casting Voodoo Love Spells 252
CHAPTER 12: CEREMONIES AND FESTIVALS 254
　　Mange Loa 255
　　Ouidah Voodoo Festival 255
　　Fat Gede 256
　　Bath of Christmas 256
　　Voodoo Fest 257
　　Gran Bois 258
　　A Voodoo Calendar 258
CONCLUSION 260
HERE'S ANOTHER BOOK BY MARI SILVA THAT YOU MIGHT LIKE 261
YOUR FREE GIFT (ONLY AVAILABLE FOR A LIMITED TIME) 262
REFERENCES 263

Part 1: Hoodoo

Unlocking the Secret Power of Rootwork, Folk Magic, Conjuration, Witchcraft, and Mojo

Introduction

Hoodoo is a subject that has been around since Africans were brought to the American shores as slaves and migrated across the country, sharing their magic and beliefs. The herbs and roots they used were amalgamated with other beliefs to form the practice we now know as Hoodoo.

Many people think that Hoodoo is a religious practice, but the truth is quite the opposite. Hoodoo isn't based on worshipping Gods, Goddesses, or other formal deities. Instead, it is a way for people to practice folk magic using the most basic tools and ingredients. So, what relevance does Hoodoo have in today's society? Quite a lot! Humans are starting to understand just what powers lie in nature and how to use them.

The natural progression to magic and rootworking rituals passed down in history seems inevitable. Understanding why some plants and herbs can attract good luck while others form a protective shield appeals to our personal sense of well-being. This type of magic and conjuring can be carried out by anyone who wants to try it, providing you respect the power and learn how to protect yourself from harm.

This book has everything you need to know to perform the craft safely and powerfully. Learn the ancient craft of Hoodoo and see how it can change your life forever!

Chapter 1: A History of Hoodoo

Hoodoo was a practice used by African slaves to retain their roots when they were transported to the Americas as slaves. Hoodoo is folk magic and incorporates the beliefs and systems of ancient African cultures alongside the Christianity that slave masters insisted were taught to their slaves. It is not a religion, although it does have its own set of deities and gods you can worship or not, depending on your preferences.

Several sources say that Hoodoo is primarily an African-based system of protection and rootwork used to guard black people against their oppressors, and it should be practiced only by Black people. More modern practitioners believe there are three different threads of Hoodoo that encompass different ethnicities. There is a Black thread of Hoodoo for people with African heritage, a White thread for European influences, and a Red thread for Native Americans. However, all humans need to be acknowledged, and their differences celebrated for the rich tapestry of Hoodoo to be seen in its entirety.

Hoodoo is a personal practice and will be used in varying ways by different people. Cultural and theological influences will influence how individuals use the rituals and rootwork to protect or enrich their lives. Ancestor veneration is a core part of Hoodoo, and the work performed is often based on historical practices.

There are no barriers to Hoodoo. People may use it to cause harm and mischief, but mostly it is used to heal and protect. The work and rituals are influenced by certain materials and talismans to signal the intentions and needs of the person performing them. A knowledge of herbs and plants and the powers they represent is essential because when it's combined with other magical elements, it works in conjunction with them.

The origins of the term hoodoo are widely disputed, but it is thought to have originated in the 17th century with the arrival of enslaved African men and women in America. During the period of slavery in the US, people from multiple ethnic groups were thrown together to work for their white masters. These included people from the Kongo, Akan, and Ewe, among many other places. These people brought with them their indigenous knowledge and beliefs that melded together to become the practice of Hoodoo.

The extent to which the slaves could practice their folk magic depended on the tolerance of their slave owners, and some regions practiced freely while others were forced to take the practice underground. A melee of beliefs and practices became the basis for this magic, and Hoodoo was used to heal and protect the slaves from their masters and bring misfortune to those that mistreated them.

What is Voodoo?

The main difference between Hoodoo and Voodoo is that Voodoo is a religion. It has specific practices, and religious leaders are required to undergo some form of ordination. In Hoodoo, there is no such formality, and everyone is free to perform the rites and rootwork that form the magical aspect of the tradition.

Voodoo has two distinct branches known as Haitian Voodoo and Louisiana or New Orleans Voodoo. There are different spellings of the word, including Vodoun or Vodou, and the two branches follow distinctly different influences.

Haitian Vodou is an African religion that traveled from the island of Haiti when members of the tribes from that area were transported into slavery and developed bonds to ensure they could depend on one another under those horrific conditions. The Lwa spirits became a focal point that all the members turned to for guidance. These included the Gede Lwa, who represented the spirits of the dead, and the Petwo Lwa, who embodied the fiery spirit of the Congo. The rituals and spells they performed involved gris-gris and magic wanga, and their liturgical language was Kreyol.

Louisiana Vodoun is distinctly different. It draws on an amalgamation of religious practices with deep spiritual roots. It shares many roots with Hoodoo but shouldn't be confused with the practice. This form of Voodoo mixes the traditional Lwa spirits of traditional Haitian Voodoo with Catholic saints and symbolism. The liturgical language used by practitioners was English with a smattering of French Creole.

Both forms of Voodoo used veves (religious symbols) and other ornately painted symbols to decorate their surroundings using cornmeal and sand to draw them on the floor. All these symbols have meaning and are related to Saints. Followers could leave offerings to the Lwa family and the related Catholic Saint on designated holidays. These veves are used to create a bridge between the spiritual and physical worlds, and when used in rituals, the participants are inviting the Lwa to take possession of their bodies for transportation purposes.

Unfortunately, racist stereotype depictions of Voodoo practices in movies and television have given both these practices a bad name. Using voodoo dolls or puppets to harm people and the casting of spells to zombify people are far from the truth. Satan doesn't play a part in Hoodoo or Voodoo. There are no pacts with the devil and no shrinking heads. Using magic dolls to cause harm to people is a European witchcraft tradition.

Hoodoo is Southern folk magic and is primarily concerned with healing and improving certain aspects of life. Healing powders and magical baths are enhanced with candles and lamps to perform spell work. These rituals are often accompanied by prayers and readings from the Bible while invoking the spirits of the Catholic saints. This type of petitioning is more personal and doesn't involve imagery or rituals.

Hoodoos Conjure Doctors and Spiritual Mothers Through the Ages

The best way to show how Hoodoo has been practiced through the years is to study some of the more famous examples of doctors or rootworkers from history.

Every rural community had a conjure doctor responsible for healing and had an ancestral knowledge of herbs, roots, and bones. They would have a bag of tricks filled with a mixture of natural and human-made items that could influence health, wealth, and prosperity. They also had the power to bring retribution to people who harmed others, which came in the form of illness or bad luck.

Historical records indicate that these types of hoodoo practitioners were born with the gift of spiritual powers and were often blessed with the gift of sight. This meant they could foretell the future and could give advice about all aspects of life. Several people believed that babies born with a caul over their head (or seventh sons or daughters) possessed certain powers.

Most conjure doctors or rootworkers inherited their powers or had them passed down through the generations. Not everybody welcomed these powers, and many saw them as a blight on their lives. There is a report of an individual named Henry Barnes, who was born in 1858 in Alabama, being born with the power of a discerning eye which meant he could see spirits. His mother decided this was a curse when her son reported seeing a cow with no head, and she set about removing his abilities. She forced her son to stir the lard when she was rendering it because she believed that cured the power of sight. Henry wrote that after stirring the lard, he didn't see spirits anymore.

Aunt Caroline Dye

Possibly the best-known sightseer of the nineteenth century, her birth name was Caroline Tracy, born in 1843 and married to her husband Martin Dye in 1867. Her legend describes her as a hoodoo woman who was a two-headed doctor, a fortune teller, and a powerful conjurer.

She would hold sessions in her Newport home and dispensed her predictions, using just a deck of cards to help her readings. She refused to deal with matters of the heart, and later in her life, she also steered clear predictions about any war or conflict (She pointedly refused to speculate on the outcome of WW1.) Aunt Caroline's reputation grew as she helped locate missing people, livestock, and personal items. She would locate areas of land that would become successful farming ventures, and it was reported that prominent businessmen wouldn't make decisions without consulting her first.

Aunt Caroline never charged for her services, but it was an unwritten rule that people who benefitted from her help would leave a few dollars as appreciation. She also received up to thirty letters a day containing pleas for her help along with monetary payments. Due to the steady traffic of people to her home, she took advantage of the situation by selling meals from her house.

Her husband died in 1907 and was buried in Gum Grove cemetery in Newport. Caroline joined him 11 years later after a short illness, and reports indicate that huge amounts of cash were found in her home. Her legacy persists as she was mentioned in two popular songs by the famous Memphis blues player, W. Handy. He mentioned a gypsy woman in both the "St Louis Blues" in 1914 and the "Sundown Blues" written nine years later. The popular African American combo known as the Memphis Jug Band also wrote a song about her called the "Aunt Caroline Dyer Blues" in the late 1920s.

Gullah Jack

Also known as Gullah Jack Pritchard, he was an African conjurer who practiced Hoodoo to attract slaves to revolt against their white slave masters in the Vesey slave conspiracy of 1822. Vesey was a carpenter and a prominent African American leader in South Carolina. He was sold as a boy into slave-hood and traveled the world with his master, Joseph Vesey. He became knowledgeable and educated, which meant he was held in regard by many of the slaves in the area.

Gullah Jack also had a reputation for leadership, and he armed the slaves with magical charms that would protect them from the buckra, the African name for white people. Pritchard and Vesey plotted to overthrow the state armory and arm local slaves to kill the white population of the city, steal their ships and return to their homelands, where slaves had already overthrown the government and where slaves now ruled.

It is easy to understand how appealing such a plot must have seemed to the slave population. Vesey had filled their heads with tales of overseas travel, and the power of his preaching combined with Pritchard's magic hoodoo powers and charms provided a heady combination for many. However, not all the slaves were loyal, and many leaked details of the revolt to their masters. Vesey, Gullah Jack, and numerous other conspirators were tried, found guilty, and subsequently hanged in July 1822.

Doctor Jim Jordan

A more recent hoodoo practitioner, James Spurgeon Jordan, was born in June 1871 and was a famous Hoodoo doctor from Como, North Carolina. He spent his whole life in his birthplace and garnered a reputation as a root doctor, gummer doctor, and all-around faith healer. In the 1890s, he began treating people with a range of diverse illnesses and was dismissed as a "trick doctor" because of his use of hoodoo imagery to impress his patients.

As his patients continued to get well, his reputation grew. Regular medical professionals and law enforcement authorities began to regard him with admiration, and he became known as an honest conjure doctor who treated his clientele with respect. He never charged for his services unless his powers had been effective and his patients were cured.

His kind disposition helped the teachings of Hoodoo become more accepted well into the 20th century. Dr. Jordan's practice underwent many significant changes during its 70-year span, and he became known for his ability to lift the shadows of ignorance and embrace the enlightened use of spiritual healing.

What Role Does Hoodoo Play in Modern Society?

Currently, we are more open to exploring spiritualism and new exciting magical avenues. We have the technology to explore different cultures and examine their teachings and beliefs. We all know how shamanism, Wicca, witchcraft and modern-day paganism, and Norse religions have risen in popularity, so surely Hoodoo can do the same.

Modern-day practitioners can embrace elements from across the world and fuse them with cultural influences depending on their location. They can take classes online and access forces to improve their lives in many ways, including monetary, health, love, and career improvements. They can also learn how to cast spells for revenge and retribution against those who have caused them harm.

The key to learning Hoodoo is to respect its history and understand the devastating foundations it came from. There was violence in the past, but that doesn't mean it can't be used for healthier outcomes in today's society. Improving your life is a powerful mission to undertake, and any form of magical or spiritual help you can gain will prove positive.

There has been a revival in the belief, thanks to people like Zora Hurston and Harry Hyatt, who worked together to preserve the beliefs and practices of Hoodoo. This led to a revival in the popularity of rootwork and magical spirituality in the early 1990s. Many modern writers have produced informative works about Hoodoo, including the popular publication Hoodoo and Conjure Quarterly, a journal describing Hoodoo and Folk Magic. Published in 2011, it is filled with historical and contemporary information about all types of magical practices and other forms of African Diaspora.

Chapter 2: Hoodoo Beliefs and Cosmology

Hoodoo is a truly eclectic form of beliefs that enables followers to embrace all forms of cultural teachings and higher beings. There are no rules, and practitioners can decide what form of Hoodooism they will practice.

Many core beliefs have turned the hodge-podge of magical practices into Hoodoo in today's recognizable form. These beliefs don't limit practitioners, but they just give them a core belief system to hold on to. They are still welcome to petition whichever higher being they choose, from the Sun god Ra to Papa Legba, as nobody judges who you choose to call on to remove obstacles and make life better.

Core Beliefs of Hoodoo Practitioners

- **The Existence of Divine Providence**

The common definition of Divine Providence is God. This is because traditional theism is based on a central figure that holds power over the universe. It tells us this divine being is responsible for all parts of creation. Hoodoo practitioners don't feel they need to follow a singular deity or a traditional idea of central power. It isn't unusual for Hoodoo followers to mix and match their deities to suit their needs. They can petition Jesus for protection in the morning while appealing to Ganesh for wisdom and call on the Mexican deity Santa Muertos to find them love.

- **Death is Not the End**

Rootworkers repeatedly call on their ancestors to help them with their daily lives, and they consult a higher plane to reach them. Hoodoo followers believe that when the physical body dies, the departed soul ascends to a higher plane to become an Ancestor. They can then be contacted by Earthbound relatives to consult with them as they offer their advice. They also intercede with the higher spirits on their behalf.

- **The Power of Clairvoyance**

The power of sight is one of the most powerful tools in a conjurer doctor's bag. The ability to see the future and communicate with disembodied spirits elevates their status in society. This form of power enables the individual to travel freely in the past and present to form a probable solution to the troubles happening in the present. The power of divination allows the participant to take an active part in others' lives and change circumstances to make the outcome better.

- **Doctrine of Signatures**

This concept is as old as mankind itself. Hoodoo teaches us there is a cosmic signature on everything in the world that indicates its intended use. Early practitioners would have to examine only a plant to understand what it should be used for.

Examples of How the Doctrine of Signatures Works

- Walnuts: These strange-looking nuts look like the human brain. Traditional healers believed that they were effective for treating head-related ailments and illnesses of the brain. Modern experts now know that the fatty acids in the nuts help improve concentration and aid memory function.

- Meadow Saffron: The roots of this plant look like a toe with gout. Incredibly, the bitter root has key ingredients like alkaloids used to treat the condition.

- Stinging nettles: The hairs on this plant look like the hairs on our heads. Traditional healers use nettles in lotions and creams to help improve blood circulation, resulting in improved hair growth. The hairs also look like animal stings, so the leaves are used to treat insect bites and stings.

- Lungwort: The white spots on this plant resemble the marks on diseased lungs, which is why the plant got its name. Healers have used it to treat tuberculosis and less dire lung conditions like coughs and asthma.

- **Retributive Justice**

Hoodoo practitioners are mainly focused on doing good and improving the lives of those around them. Most religions and practices embrace the philosophy of doing no harm to others, and no harm will befall you. Hoodoo differs, as it believes in the biblical principle of an "eye for an eye" and allows people to demand justice to fit the crime. This measured form of retribution will often take the form of inflicting illness and pain on the recipient but rarely involves more fatal outcomes.

- **Intention**

In certain belief systems, there is the power to curse and hex others, depending on the power of the person laying the curse. Hoodoo followers believe that such curses and jinxes will only work if the person they are directed at is deserving of the hex. Many Hoodoo practices involve powders labeled with intentions. These can include the following.

- Boss Fix powder designed to bring your boss into line

- Confusion powder designed to bring chaos to those working against you

- Court case powder is used to influence the judge and jury to find in your favor.

- Devils shoestring sachet used to restrain your enemies and restrict their movements.

- Hotfoot sachets to drive people from your life

For instance, the Boss Fix powder will only work on your boss and won't affect other people who work with you. Furthermore, it will only work if your boss is a bad one. If it doesn't work, then you may be a bad employee! The Court Case powder will only work for innocent parties and is not intended to get a favorable verdict for guilty parties.

This belief system stems from the Bible and, more specifically, Proverbs 26.2, which states, *"Like a fluttering sparrow or a darting swallow an undeserved curse will not come to rest."* Nobody receives a curse without reason, according to Hoodoo's beliefs.

One of the lesser-known influences in Hoodoo beliefs originates in Germany. The sixth and seventh Book of Moses has over 125 articles that can be used in magical practices. Hexenfoos listed in the books are powerful talismans and symbols that protect against even the most powerful forms of curses and hexes. They can be painted on cradles to protect babies and other household objects to protect the people who live there.

Legend tells of God dictating this detailed guide to witchcraft to Moses as he resided on Mount Sinai, but it was omitted from the Old Testament because of its power. The book's contents were then passed down through the ages until it reached King Solomon, who used the guide to become one of the most powerful figures in Christianity.

Immigrants brought German-language editions of this text to America, where it became part of Hoodoo legend. The traditional healers and conjure doctors of the early 19th century used the working spells and accompanying necromancy to enhance the rootwork they were using.

To summarize, Hoodoo has a set of principles that most of us would like to adhere to. Even if the magical aspects of the tradition don't appeal, the root beliefs might help you form a new set of intentions to adhere to.

What is the Spiritual Meaning of Stars?

The night skies have been a source of fascination since the beginning of time. The celestial bodies that twinkle above our heads were mysterious, and even with the knowledge we have today, they are still a source of wonder for humankind. Imagine how appealing the stars and planets must have looked to slaves who had no sense of freedom and were shackled to their work and masters.

It isn't surprising that, like many mythological, religious, and spiritual systems, the followers of Hoodoo looked to the cosmos to enhance their beliefs and connect with higher powers. Astrology and the connection to the stars begin with the term astrology. It is derived from two Greek words, Astron and logos, which translate as "a star" "that is said," which seems to suggest that the stars contain the word of God.

Astrology is not a mainstream technique used in Hoodoo. The phases of the moon and the signs of the Zodiac were often used to affect the timing of rootwork and other spells.

Intentions Dictated by Signs of the Zodiac

1) Aries: The house of self. The period of a new moon in Aries is all about changing yourself and your approach.

2) Taurus: The house of money. Now is the time to set intentions regarding wealth and income.

3) Gemini: The house of travel and commuting. Gemini is the perfect sign to begin new journeys. Start a new project and

increase the chance of success by setting your intentions when the moon is in Gemini.

4) Cancer; The house of family. Set intentions to form stronger family bonds and contact people who have moved away or relocated. When the new moon is in Cancer, it's time to clean your house and get rid of clutter. Clear the physical space, and your mental strength will benefit.

5) Leo: The house of love. When the moon is in this sector, it's time to get those love potions working. Attract a new partner or starting a new project will work, and couples trying for a child will conceive more successfully during a new moon.

6) Virgo: The house of work. Intentions regarding your career or seeking new work will be auspicious in his period. This is also a good time to work on yourself, start a new health regime, and improve your diet and exercise routines.

7) Libra: The house of relationships. When the new moon is in the house of Libra, it signals the time to work on your connections. This includes your personal and business relationships. Try to strengthen the existing ties you may have neglected lately.

8) Scorpio: The house of an enigma. When the moon is in the eighth house, it's time to set intentions surrounding shared resources. Practical applications involve paying off debts and resolving tax issues so you can begin to start saving for future projects.

9) Sagittarius: The house of knowledge. This is an opportune time to expand your horizons and embrace new subjects. Take an online course about something that is completely outside your normal remit and would never have appealed to you before. Plan a trip to somewhere different, maybe swap a beach resort for more cultural breaks.

10) Capricorn: The house of the public. Now it's time to work on your image. This could mean updating your CV or improving your online presence. Be visible in the workplace, and you are receiving the recognition you deserve.

11) Aquarius: The house of friendship. Take the time and set intentions to meet new people. Network in different groups and increase your social interactions. This will help with work and personal life.

12) Pisces: The house of the hidden. Discover your inner self and use this time to meditate and find your inner peace. Set intentions to work on yourself and say no to other people. This is not a selfish outlook, and it just means you need to concentrate on nurturing yourself for once.

Hoodoo oils are especially connected to astrological timings. Using specific oils during the different phases of the moon will increase their effectiveness on the person using them.

While the Zodiac is important, other astral signs are also significant in the teachings of Hoodoo. The stars are one of the earliest forms of guidance, and Hoodoo's followers are no different. They represent divine energy that all people can direct their intentions toward. Their physical distance represents hard to achieve goals and reminds people they need to try harder and work toward their divine purposes. The symbolic meaning of the stars is complex and vast. They represent the powers of the divine beings and represent the concept of greatness and cosmic enlightening.

The Morning and the Evening Stars

While they have separate names, these two astral stars are actually the same celestial body. Because they were seen at different times, it was believed that they were two bodies and were named as such.

When the Morning Star rises, it leads the Sun into the sunrise and is seen as a leading light that brings knowledge and power. As the Sun sets in the evening, it can be seen shining brightly beside it before they both disappear behind the horizon. Many cultures believe this star is the embodiment of the fallen angel, Lucifer, whose name represents the personification of the light bringer.

Shooting Stars

Different cultures interpret falling stars in various ways. It can herald a change in fortune and an extremely positive omen or signal a fallen angel. Asian cultures see the appearance of a shooting star as a bad and negative omen, and Hoodoo followers interpret both meanings depending on the circumstances.

Solomon's Pentagram

Often the pentagram is associated with black magic and negative forces, but historically the opposite is true. Hoodoo followers have used this astral symbol to set intentions for generations. There are hundreds of combinations to promote blessings, love, and wealth and to punish wrongdoings. Combined with other pentacle signs and symbols, Solomon's pentagram is the ultimate sign of power and wisdom.

Modern practitioners will design their pentacles and pentagrams using traditional seals and symbols alongside more modern images.

A Brief Guide to Important Signs From Cosmology

- To enhance the power of the Sun, use a point within a circle
- A triangle is both a symbol of the Sun and the alchemic symbol of fire
- A crescent moon is a symbol for both the moon and water. This symbol will protect you from evil and bring good luck
- A triangle with a line across the base represents air
- The same triangle for air inverted represents the Earth

Using these basic symbols combined with other representations of your character and specifics will make your seal or symbol a true logo of your intentions.

Elements That Can be Included

- Your zodiac signs
- Your Chinese Zodiac signs
- Your preferred totem animals
- Your birthstones
- Favorite colors
- Preferred numbers
- Numerical birth number

The key to designing a logo that works in your Hoodoo practices is to have fun and just use the elements that appeal to you. The universe comprises amazing materials that will inspire you and fill your work with power.

Chapter 3: The Hoodoo Toolkit: Ingredients and Materials

Now it's time to get your hands dirty, literally! The Hoodoo practices and spells often include dirt and dust, which were readily available to all the practitioners no matter where they were. This type of ingredient is one of the most important hoodoo magic components and is known as *Goofer dust*.

What is Goofer Dust?

The name derives from the Bantu word kufua, which means "to die," and it is used to harm or kill the targeted victim. Composed primarily from graveyard dirt and dust, it also incorporates other ingredients depending on the required outcome. Snakeskin and salt are added to the dust to create a powerful way to cause someone harm.

The Goofer dust is spread on the victim's pillow or around the path they use to cause the greatest damage. The first sign the hex has worked is sharp pains in the legs or feet followed by severe swelling, which leads to the inability to walk. The term has also evolved to become a verb and a noun. The term "goofering someone" refers to any practice that involves a form of poisoning or inflicting harm by introducing injurious elements into their environment.

In January 2016, a man from Queens was sentenced to 50 years in prison for killing his parents five years earlier. After firing four sets of defense lawyers, he represented himself in court and claimed that his parents died as a direct result of his mother's use of goofer dust in the home. The truth was that he bludgeoned his mother to death and choked her with a pearl necklace before plunging her head into the bathtub.

Graveyard Dirt

Dirt and dust are different things. The dirt from graveyards is the actual soil surrounding the grave, while the dust is residual material found on the surface. The Bokongo people of Central Africa are believed to be the source of this form of magic, and they believed that the dirt contained the spirits of the people buried in the soil. When they traveled to America in 1730 as slaves, they brought this concept with them.

Graveyard dirt can't just be taken. It needs to be purchased. This involves communing with the dead person and creating a contract to buy the dirt. This would usually involve the purchaser leaving a gift on the grave for the deceased, usually in something they enjoyed in life, like liquor or money.

Not all graveyard dirt is equal. The dirt from the graves of babies and young children is especially powerful for healing and spells of good fortune, while the dirt from directly above the heart of the body is used for love spells. If you plan more iniquitous deeds, then the dirt from a murderer's grave will prove more powerful. Dirt from the graves of lesser criminals can be used to cast spells of chaos and disorder.

Plants and Herbs of Hoodoo

As with any form of witchcraft and magic, a major part of your toolkit will consist of natural materials like plants and herbs.

Here are a couple of the more powerful tools nature supplies for hoodoo magic:

- **The Rose of Jericho**

This is a Mexican plant that is also called the resurrection plant and the false plant. It is brown and brittle when dry, but when immersed in water, it unfurls and becomes a vibrant green sacred plant that is perfectly geometrical. Spells cast with this plant involve resurrecting an old love or creating love where there was none before.

- **Horsetail**

This verdant plant grows in humid environments and is known for its magical and medicinal properties. When harvested correctly, it is used to cleanse the body as it has beneficial fungicides, but it can be toxic if harvested at the wrong time.

- **Basil**

In Hoodoo, basil is used as a magnet of fortune. Adding this bright leafy herb makes a spell more powerful as a love potion or an inducement for prosperity. Basil can also be used to ward off evil spirits and bad vibes. More practically, it can help keep mosquitoes at bay.

- **John the Conqueror Root**

This is a staple part of Hoodoo rituals, and its powers can be traced back to early African American folklore. The story tells of the son of an African King named John the Conquer, who fell in love with the devil's daughter Lilith. The devil tried to trick John by setting him a task to win his daughter's hand, but John outwitted the devil and escaped to Africa with Lilith and the devil's magic horse.

It is this power of trickery and success that John is believed to have left behind in the Americas in this powerful root. You only have to possess the plant to benefit from the powers of luck and love it contains, and the essence of the root is used to bring power to candles, crystals, and sachets. Carry dried root with the hair of someone you love to draw their admiration and interest.

High John soaps and shower gels can refresh the body and build levels of confidence. They can also help you score on a hot date! You can make your own or buy them from commercial sites like luckshop.com who offer bars of soap for $5 that promise to raise your inner vibrations and strengthen your resolve.

- **Palo Santo**

This is one of the most powerful and sacred plants on Earth. Found in areas of South America, it is used to burn as a cleanser by shamans and other healers across the world. It can also be used to make herbal teas that will purify the body and improve the immune system. While it isn't commonly available, it can be sourced from traditional medicinal shops and apothecaries. It is available in resin, oil, or wood form and used as an essential oil to make fragrant steam.

- **Cinnamon**

This is an extremely useful, readily available part of your hoodoo tool kit. It is used for sexual arousal spells, and burning it when having sex is said to enhance the experience.

Cinnamon also attracts wealth, prosperity, and cleansing. Cinnamon tea is used to treat gastronomic problems and relieving sickness and vomiting. Cinnamon is often used as a protection tool when placed in doorways and windows in the home.

- **Plants Used to Attract Wealth**

There aren't many people who would turn down the chance to have more money or wealth, so many Hoodoo practices are centered on attracting wealth.

These plants will help your spells attract the prosperity you seek:

The money plant: Also known as the golden pothos, this plant should be placed around any sharp angles within the house to purify the home and make it a place for success.

The mother-in-law plant: Also known as the snake plant, this healthy plant provides a natural source of moisture and cleanliness.

Crassula: These vibrant plants have succulent leaves and are used to bring financial abundance to your home. They should be placed in the southeast corners of your home.

Bamboo: Asian cultures have used this plant for generations to bring good health and luck, and hoodoo practitioners have also embraced its qualities. Lucky bamboo is a genus of the plant used to bring blessings to you and your household.

Jasmine: The aroma this plant conjure attracts money and luck when placed around the home. It is also considered an aphrodisiac so that you can get rich and lucky simultaneously.

Sage: All good pagans know the power of sage and how it cleans and refreshes energy. Hoodoo is no different, and its healing properties are used to bring love and good luck to spells and potions.

Chamomile: This daisy-like plant is known for its calming effect and healing properties. When used in Hoodoo, it attracts wealth and power.

Bayberry: Grown in the East of the US, this is a shrub with dark bark and berries used to make medicine. When dried and blended, it attracts love and prosperity.

Hoodoo Tools

Actual tools have no magical powers without the spiritual intent of the user. They provide a medium to direct the spirituality and power that lies with the Hoodoo practitioner. Some people will find the powerful, while others will need just the barest essentials to practice their craft.

There is a wealth of choice when it comes to choosing your particular bag of tricks, and some items are fun to own even if they aren't used in magical rituals.

Amulets and Charms

These items are used to produce vibrations and energies for the holder and the recipient of magic. They often have daily functions, yet they become magical in the right hands. Candles and holders play a significant role in certain hoodoo rituals, and it is important to have a stock of them in various colors.

Many of the most effective amulets are formed by the user and contain personal effects like hair and nail clippings to give them extra power. There are several powerful talismans connected to luck, and that are carried by gamblers and poker players. Most of these contain symbols originating from the Key of Solomon and attract power, success, and wealth.

Coyote Claws

Coyotes are known for their trickster ways, and stories tell of them stealing fire from the gods to give it to mankind, setting his tail on fire during the raid, which accounts for the markings on their tail.

Although the coyote is a rogue, he has mankind's best interest at heart. He can travel in the dark and find water in desolate places. His claw is carried by scouts and travelers who want to benefit from his skills and remain undiscovered when traveling. Claws can be purchased from select online hoodoo suppliers.

Porcupine Needles

These American needles are fun to use and can be incorporated in candles, dolls, and rootwork. They provide protection and should be placed around the object that needs protecting with the black pointy bit facing outward.

Incense

Burning incense when performing spells and rituals enhances the experience and signals the intention of the practitioner. Use a clay burning bowl to burn your incense and self-igniting charcoal to fuel the flame.

Blends of Incense and What They Promote

- African juju: Used to draw passion and intense desire into a relationship.

- Banishing: Remove unwanted and harmful people from your life by burning this incense when casting your spells.

- Chuparosa: Also known as hummingbird incense, burn it to draw your lover closer like a hummingbird seeking nectar.

- Dragon's blood: Containing the real blood of dragons, this resin should be burned to bring power and strength when performing rituals.

- Has no Hanna: This incense should be used to enhance your tools. Pass them through the smoke to enhance, charge and reenergize them before use.

- Jinx killer: This special blend of incense is burned to give protection from all hexes and curses sent your way.

- Obeah: This incense is burned by sorcerers and rootworkers who wish to communicate with the spirits.

- Seven African Powers: This orisha essence is used to obtain energy from Africa's seven saints.

- Tranquility: Burned to bring peace and harmony to your home.

Lucky Hoodoo products Inc. creates and blends these incense products and many more. If you don't see the product you require, ask them to blend the formula to suit your needs. Prices range between $9 and $30 for 2 oz tins.

Crossing Products

Sometimes you need to take the gloves off and fight your enemies with powerful rootwork. You can use your herbs and other ingredients to blend your own formulas, or you can buy oils and powders ready-made from online sources.

Black Arts Oil

This is one of the most powerful blends in Hoodoo. It is used to cross up or curse your enemies who have caused harm to you or your loved ones. You can create your oil using baneful substances like snakeskin, red pepper, and sulfur mixed with the herbs you prefer, or you can buy ready mixed oil online.

Boss Fix Oil

When the hoodoo community wanted to "give it to the man" or give their boss a taste of their wrath, they would concoct a fixing oil or powder to cause discomfort when they touched certain objects like keys or doorknobs. Mixtures containing licorice, high john herbs, and other powerful herbs were used to pay back bosses who were less than kind to their staff.

This type of oil or powder can be used in modern workplaces and can be sprinkled onto their office doorknob or computer keyboard. Recite an accompanying prayer to stop them from micromanaging you and realize what a key worker you are.

Poppets

These traditional dolls are often mistaken for voodoo dolls that represent other people and that are used to cause pain. In hoodoo practices, poppets are formed from cloth or wax and represent a spirit connected to the owner. There is no malice intended when a poppet is formed, and if you treat your doll well, it will do the same for you.

When making your poppet, the color of the fabric you use will determine the powers it holds. They can be made from simple white felt and then added to, or you can choose a hue from the list below to imbue your poppet with magic:

Banishing: Black fabric decorated with swords or fire.

Ingenuity: Use orange or yellow fabrics with bright symbols like the sun or fire.

Healing: Use spiritual colors like pale blue or white and decorate with clouds and stars.

Love and passion: Red or deep pink fabric decorated with hearts and bows.

Wealth: Silver or gold fabric with green trims. Decorate with dollar bills or coins and cups.

Protection: Red or white material decorated with shields or keys. Use mistletoe to add an extra layer of protection.

Other Tools That Are Part of Hoodoo Lore

Lodestones

Naturally occurring magnetized pieces of iron ore lodestones are used to draw positive influences toward the user. They attract love and money and are also used to direct spells away from the practitioner who has been cast by others.

Lucky Blue Balls

Known as anil in Latin American countries, these bright blue spheres are made from copper sulfate and carried for good luck. When dissolved in water, they provide a cleansing solution that will protect your house and make it a lucky place to live.

Pyrite

Known as fool's gold, this shiny mineral is widely used in Hoodoo to draw money and success to the person who carries it. Small chunks of the material can be bought for as little as $10 and make a perfect accompaniment for important attraction spells.

Coins

Certain coins play roles in Hoodoo and are often silver dollars or souvenir good luck coins. These will often have a personal attachment to the person who carries them. In the 1930s, at the height of the Great Depression, these coins were manufactured to bring luck to people who were suffering. They feature horseshoes, four-leaf clover, and other symbols of good luck.

Most of the coins have no monetary value and can be found online or in traditional shops selling hoodoo paraphernalia.

Mojo Beans

Also known as wishing beans and African mojo beans, these are classic good luck talismans and should be carried in a piece of red material to bring the holder good fortune.

Twice Stricken Lightning Wood

This is a popular tool in Hoodoo and is a powder ground from wood that has been struck by lightning. It has powers of attraction that can be used for sexual spells and commanding a lover to return. It also has cleansing properties as the lightning represents the power of purity and transformation.

Bones

Throwing the bones is one of the most traditional forms of divination and is part of hoodoo-style worship. The bones used will all have a meaning, and how the throw is interpreted will depend on the person who casts them. The bone reader should cast a petition to the gods describing what they need to know before casting the bones to the mat or animal skin covering a table.

Many people believe that the further away the bones fall means they depict things from the future while the closest bones relate to the present. Spaces between the bones or the shapes they make all have relevance.

If you intend to perform this divination rite, it is important to have a variety of natural bones and other objects to cast. Include items like:

- The arm from a china doll
- Alligator foot
- Sharks' tooth
- Dog ankle bone
- Shell from nutmeg
- Snake vertebra
- Raccoon penis bone
- Rabbit rib bone
- Abalone shell
- Cowrie shell
- Vintage keys
- Ravens' claw
- Chickens' foot

This is just a selection of items you can use to throw the bones. Add jewelry or personal items to make the reading more relevant to whoever wants their questions answered.

Chapter 4: Spiritual Cleansing Basics

Your Hoodoo toolkit may seem like the most important part of your practical work, but you also need to keep your tools and home clean. They need to be physically clean, but more importantly, they – and you –should be spiritually clean.

The ingredients you need will differ depending on your requirements and methods, but there are some standard components in a Hoodoo cleansing kit. Spiritual cleansing is important for many reasons. It allows you to perform at your best, and it banishes any negative energies that may attach themselves to yourself and your environment. Think of these cleansing rituals as being the spiritual equivalent of washing your hands and brushing your teeth. They need to be done regularly and thoroughly.

What You Need to Have in Your Cleaning Kit

- Candles
- Salt
- Brick dust
- Graveyard dirt

- Chicken or turkey wing
- Chicken foot
- Crystals
- Herbs like sage, rosemary, sweetgrass, and palo santo
- Holy or blessed water
- Essential oils
- Natural bath salts
- Alcohol rub

Personal Cleansing

This form of ritual is especially important if you are feeling under the weather or anxious about something. If you feel like your powers are waning and you have blockages in your aura, then cleansing your body and soul will help you restore your energy levels.

Cleansing is one of the most important parts of conjure work, and it's essential to make time for your rituals. To get the best results to perform the cleansing during certain planetary hours. This will increase the powers of your ritual and give them added intentions. Use an online planetary hour calculator to calculate the body that rules the day and choose the best day for you.

Ritual baths are the perfect way to cleanse your aura and feel the power of your magic for hours after. If you feel that negative energies stop you from being yourself, draw a hot bath, add natural bath salts, drops of essential oil (citrus oils like lemongrass and ylang-ylang are perfect), add two cups of blessed water, and sprinkle with your favorite herbs. Light two white candles and place them at the side of your bath. Add the ingredients as the bath fills to energize the atmosphere, and when it is filled, step in.

Now take a jug and pour the water over your head 13 times while reciting a cleansing prayer. Psalm 37 is a prayer option, or you can compose your own prayer. Only wash downward, so negative energies are flushed into the bathwater. Once you feel refreshed and cleansed, step out of the bath, and air dry yourself (no drying with towels) before dressing in clean clothes. Now take a jug full of the bathwater before draining the rest. Take your saved bathwater and head for a crossroads. Throw the water over your shoulder and then walk back home without looking back. If you are lucky enough to have trees in your garden, you can dispose of the bathwater by throwing it at the trunk so it can absorb the negativity.

Handy tip: This type of bath can be used as an attraction bath with a few simple changes. Use the same ingredients but add rose petals or other floral essential oils to your water. Wash in an upward manner and pour the water over your head 7 or 9 times. Recite Psalm 23 or other uplifting text while you wash and then air dry yourself before dressing. Using yellow or red candles will make the object of your attraction more attainable, and the saved water should be used to wash your front doorstep and be swept inwards to bring the attraction toward you.

Quick-Fix Methods of Cleansing Yourself

If you can't use baths to cleanse yourself because you don't have the time, or you just need a quick fix, you can use several of the following methods to remove negativity.

The chicken foot: This is a wonderful tool for cleansing, and lightly scratching yourself with it will keep your energy positive and will remove any negative energies. Think how the chicken deals with its mess. It simply scratches it away and moves on!

Brushing: If you feel like your cleansing should be more rigorous, but you want to use natural elements, then upgrade to a turkey or chicken wing. If you feel the need to remove a crossing or a jinx, take the turkey wing and brush it down from the top of your head to the base of your feet. Traditionally turkeys gobble up all the mess, so the wing will remove the condition and cleanse your aura.

Rubdown

Use your alcohol rub to form a base. Add herbs and oils to infuse the mixture before rubbing yourself down. Perform the ritual in a sacred place and use prayers and spiritual chants to enhance the experience.

Candle Cleansing

Use a black candle to remove a crossed or jinxed condition. Wipe yourself with the candle in downward movements while praying.

Smoke Cleansing

Also known as smudging, this process can be performed by burning incense, essential oils, or dried herbs. Use a white cloth to cover yourself from the neck down and burn the selected items under it. Allow the smoke to swirl around you before removing the sheet and allowing the smoke to permeate the house.

Sprinkle

Use a sprinkler head to perform this ritual. Fill it with holy or blessed water and add salt and essential oils to the liquid. Sprinkle your head and shoulders with the water, recite your favorite psalm (psalm 23 works well), and then sprinkle your feet.

Cleansing and Blessing the Home

Floor washes based on the elements used in cleansing baths can be used to clean houses and other physical places. The same rule of directing energies applies to floor washes, just like it applies to bathing. Wash windows and doors downward to dispel negativity and upward to attract goods, luck, and wealth. Candles, prayers, and smudging can all be used to give your cleanse added depth.

Hoodoo practitioners will often use elemental ingredients to increase the power of their house cleanses and blessings. Here are a few ways to use these strong influences in your rituals:

Earth

Actual dirt is the most basic elemental form of Earth, but not everyone wants to have dirt on their floor. Several substitutes can be used just as effectively.

- Redbrick dust: Hoodoo practitioners believe this form of Earth is particularly effective, and they will sprinkle it almost everywhere. Doorways and windows, thresholds, and entrances should all be protected, and red brick dust does the job perfectly. The most powerful dust is from old houses or sacred buildings, and homemade dust can be found almost everywhere. There are specialist spiritual products online, but ensure they are reputable and the dust has provenance.

Lay unbroken lines across your thresholds to form psychic barriers that are impossible to cross. The most effective time to perform this ritual is the eve of the full moon, and the dust should be replaced monthly.

- Salt: Salt is readily available and can be removed only by evaporation. Sea salt is particularly effective, and many Hoodoo practitioners swear by the salt from the Dead Sea. Salt or saltwater can be used to solve problems with nightmares and bad dreams. Sprinkle the area around the bed with salt to remove nighttime influences and aid healthy sleep. A box filled with sea salt at your front door will protect your home and stop negative energy from entering.

- Black salt: This is a mixture of regular or sea salt with iron filings or charcoal. This type of salt should be used when obstructions or negative energies are particularly strong.

Air

This element is incorporated naturally in house blessings and cleanses. Burning candles or incense permeates the air while doors and windows can be opened to allow negativity to escape.

Fire

Both black and white candles bring power to your cleansing. Their potency is increased when combined with essential oils like Myrrh or Sandalwood. Use burners to protect and clean doorways and windows.

Water

Most deep cleanses are based around the element water, and it is used to wash away a multitude of ills. You can ask your local church for blessed water, or it can be purchased online.

Alternatively, You Can Bless Your Own Water With the Following Method

Step 1: Collect seawater for your cleanse. If you take it from natural sources, be sure to leave a gift for the spirits that live there. A small offering of fresh fruit or vegetables will show you are thankful for their blessings.

Step 2: Gather rainwater. Use open containers to collect fresh rainwater from your garden or windowsill. Water gathered during a thunderstorm is particularly effective. The morning dew is also used for rituals to bring revitalization to your home.

Step 3: Make your water holy

There are Hoodoo practitioners that believe in the power of moonlight, and leaving your water outside overnight renders it holy. Mix the seawater and rainwater and place the mix in a silver or glass container. Place the container on a table in the garden where it will receive the most exposure to moonlight. Charge the water with your blessings and prayers before you leave it.

Other practitioners believe that prayer is the most powerful way to create holy water. Use readings and prayers from your favored texts and religious teachings to bless your water. A simple way to do this is to say, *"Water is the giver of life, and I ask the powers of the spiritual world to bless it and make it holy. I call upon the Gods and Goddesses to infuse this water with love, purity, and peace."*

Step 4: Add salt

Ideally, you will use a form of holy salt. Use the same phrase as you did for the water but replace the phrase "giver of life" with "preserver of life" to consecrate your salt and make it more powerful.

Step 5: Combine the two elements. Add pinches of salt to the water while stirring in a clockwise direction. Say the final prayer, *"This holy union is blessed with the power of the elements and life. The Gods and Goddesses have made this union powerful and ready to be used in goodness and health."*

Cleansing Spells for Toxicity

The modern world is filled with sources of negative energy. The environment we occupy is prone to toxins and negativity, so sometimes we need to clear specific areas of frustration and negativity. These spells are designed to focus on intentions rather than perform a general cleansing ritual.

Moonlight Spell

You will need:

- Incense
- Calming music
- White candle

Step 1: On the evening of a full moon, take a cleansing bath before air-drying yourself and dressing in a white robe.

Step 2: Find a calm relaxing place outdoors or in front of a window that allows you to see the moon.

Step 3: Play your music and light your incense.

Step 4: Call upon the spirit who guards you, this can be a God or Goddess, or you can call on your angel you feel an affinity toward or your guardian angel.

Step 5: Ask them to protect your soul's energy and fill you with their healing powers.

Step 6: Feel the energy flow into you from the base of your feet to the top of your head.

Step 7: Forgive yourself for being human; feeling the pressures of the world begin to overcome your emotions.

Step 8: Thank the universe for its blessings and your individual angel or spirit for their help.

Spell for the Soul

If you feel that your soul is heavy and the world is taking over, regain your control by performing this powerful spell.

You will need:
- White candle
- Blessed water
- Holy salt
- Dried sage
- Bowl for burning herbs

Step 1: Choose a night during a waning moon to perform the ritual.

Step 2: Light the candle and invite the spirits to bless your endeavors.

Step 3: Quickly move your hand through the candle flame while reciting the following phrase *"I use this fire to release the negative energies within me, and I ask they are replaced with good intentions."*

Step 4: Rub the holy salt into your hands and say, *"Through this earthly element, I relinquish all obstacles and elements of negativity in my life."*

Step 5: Now burn your dried sage in the bowl. Breathe in the smoke and say, *"With the element Air, I cleanse my soul and remove all troubling thoughts."*

Step 6: Plunge your hands into the water and say, *"I use the element water to release my toxins and bring clear intentions to my soul."*

Now take the time to enjoy your newly charged soul and fill your thoughts with the future you will have.

Step 7: Dispose of the ingredients by mixing the salt with the ashes and dissolving it in the water. Bury the mixture at the base of a tree or scatter it at a crossroads.

These types of rituals are designed so you can customize them to suit your needs and requirements. Just like Hoodoo itself, the rituals and cleanses are made to be powerful extensions of your beliefs. If you have a strong bond with Catholicism, the holy water process will differ from the one described here. Listen to your heart and soul and be led by your instincts.

Chapter 5: Creating a Mojo Bag

One of the simplest ways to make your magic practices more effective and personally charged is by using a mojo bag to carry your charms and magical tools. They are also called gris-gris bags, toby, conjuring sacks, and condition bags.

You can have as many mojo bags as you like, and tailoring them to suit your needs is simple. Think of your mojo bags as batteries for your powers that need recharging regularly and should always be carried with you. There are many commercial types of bags available, but a handmade one will help you connect to your magical sources. Creating your bag is simple but satisfying, and the objects you place within them are paramount to the success of your intentions.

Hands-on involvement with ritual work enhances the power you create, so if you can hand sew the bag with colored thread and use decorative ribbon, you will be investing part of yourself into the bag. This will increase the effectiveness of its contents and lift the energy they emit.

Color is a major factor when choosing the fabric for your bags, but the material is also important. Rich velvets and satins work well for some, while others will prefer muslin or cotton materials.

Remember, you know what suits you and what your bag will be used for. Treat your mojo bag as an extension of your character, and it will serve you well.

Colors to Choose for Your Mojo Bag

- Gold: This works with the Sun and encourages wealth and success combined with projectivity. The god yang is linked with gold, and he provides a loud, in-your-face type of energy.

- Silver: Working with the moon, the goddess yin is linked with this color and promotes meditative processes and peace.

- Red: Connected to the planet Mars, passion and courage are associated with this hue. The deeper the red, the more energetic the mojo.

- Orange: Associated with the planet Mercury, orange is the color of success. It helps give the ingredients of the bag the power of vitality and speed.

- Yellow: Governed by the Sun, yellow is the color of joy and creativity. Bring an aura of allure to your spells when you store your tools in this bag.

- Green: working with the planet Venus your bag will be imbued with the power of good fortune and wealth.

- Blue: Associated with the planet Jupiter use blue material to bring wisdom and rhetoric to your spells. This is the color of intelligence and represents the deep connection you have mentally with the spirits.

- Violet: This striking color is all about healing and aiding karmic connections. Tools kept in this bag will be powerful when connecting to the spiritual world or using divination connections.

- Rose Pink: This is the color of love and friendship. Use it to enhance your romantic and creative skills and increase personal beauty.

- White: The classic color of divination and spirituality. This bag will help you connect to angels and improve your psychological health.

- Grey: Objects stored in grey bags will become mysterious and will be powerful when creating illusions. They will be powerful in spells involving invisibility and secretive moves.

- Black: Banishing spells and protection rituals will work better with a black mojo bag. The planet Saturn is associated with this color and provides a level of discipline.

Make Your Bag

Step One

Measure and cut your fabric so it forms a rectangle roughly three times as wide as it is long. For instance, 12 inches long and 4 inches wide.

Step Two

Fold the fabric in half so that the smooth side of the fabric is facing inward. Carefully position the ends and edges and, if necessary, trim any stray strands of fabric.

Step Three

Sew the sides of the bag, leaving the last two inches unsown, so it forms a pocket. Keep the stitching small and neat and leave the top of the bag open as this will be your opening.

Step Four

Turn your bag inside out, so the smooth side of the fabric is showing, and your stitches are hidden. Fold down the unsown fabric so it forms a flap on both sides of your bag.

Step Five

Take your scissors and carefully make four small incisions along the fold you have just created.

Step Six

Take a ribbon or colored string and thread it through the slits you have just created. Make sure the cord is long enough to encompass the neck of your bag with extra for tying.

Step Seven

Charge your bag. Place crystals, stones, herbs, and other items to make your bag fit the purpose it is meant for.

Step Eight

Draw the string tight and keep your items safe within.

Now you need to choose the objects you place in your bag. What goes in is determined by your goal and what is a proven way to achieve that goal. There will always be at least one item in your bag, and often it will come with others. Traditionally there should be an odd number of things in your bag as even numbers are considered passive while odd numbers are active and dynamic. There should never be over 13; however, as a result, it will be less effective if the bag is overfilled.

Now you need to load your bag with pertinent items. Corresponding herbs, stones, and amulets can be used along with personal objects that signal your intentions.

- For protection, use lodestone, obsidian arrowheads, basil, and a protective amulet.
- For good luck, fill your bag with dried John the Conqueror root, a rabbit foot, three-leaf clover, and lucky coins.
- For wealth and success, place a lodestone alongside John the Conqueror root with tumbled tiger eye crystals and a selenite stick.
- For love, place rosehip and magnetized sand with dried petals and rose quartz heart crystals alongside a piece of paper with a love declaration in your bag.

- For lifting a hex or crossing a jinx, put dried poke root with an alligator claw, magnetized salt, and moss agate crystal in your bag.

Once loaded, it's time to bless your bag. Blow into your open bag and repeat a prayer to bless your items. Say, *"With my breath, I bless you just like the Lord blew breath into all of us and gave us life"* Draw the cord tight and make sure your bag is secure. Use magic oil to anoint your bag with five dots or sprays. Place a dot at each corner and one in the center.

Hold your bag in your hands and repeat the phrase *"I bless you and set you a purpose, (now state that purpose) and I bind you and give you the strength to be successful."*

Now fix your purpose with a magic candle. Take nine pins and a candle and write your purpose on the candle before you impale the nine pins into it. The last pin should be inserted through the wick just before you light it and state your intention again. If you are creating a mojo, you can't overstate your intentions. Every affirmation will increase the chances of success.

Now you need to name your mojo bag and make it the physical body representing your spiritual ally. True hoodoo practitioners don't see their mojo bags as an inanimate talisman. Your mojo is part of you and, because of this, should be named. Consider it from a psychological view, the name you give your bag will help you associate a personality and energy with it, and you will begin to view your bags as friends and allies.

Tips to Help You Name Your Bag

- Listen to your heart. Once you have made your bag, you will begin to hear certain names or see a sign that indicates what to call your bag. You may dream of meeting a woman called Mary and then see the name in the press a couple of times. This will help you decide what to call your bag.

- You may decide to name the bag after yourself. For instance, if your name is Peter, you can use Little Pete or Petey. Derivations of your name make the bag more personal, but you will run out of them depending on how many bags you make.

- For a more off-the-wall name, you need to pick a person who symbolizes the endeavor you want your bag to represent. For instance, if you want to attract wealth, call your bag Elon or Bezos after the tech giants. Love mojo bags should be called Romeo or Cupid to signify their connection to romance. The base idea is your bag will take on the characteristics of the person after whom it is named.

- Look to your faith. If you are of a certain faith, then biblical names will be suitable. Samson is a great name for strength, while Adam means living. Research your choices with a baby name book to discover what different names mean.

- Let the spirits guide you. Take a random book from your bookshelf and let it fall open. There will be a name there that shouts to you and tells you what to call your bag.

Once your bag is loaded, blessed, and named, it's time to make it part of your being. For the first week, your need to keep it close to your skin. Pin it inside your clothes or wear it around your neck so it can imbue your spirit and become part of your psyche. At night pin it to the base of your pillow or keep it on your nightstand. Feed it with magic oil regularly during that first week and keep it dry and clean.

How Long Does the Mojo Bag Work?

Most bags will remain powerful for a year. There are a few guidelines to follow to keep your bag working:

1) Your bag is for your eyes only. If someone else sees or touches your bag, it can "kill your hand" and render the mojo inactive.

2) Hard items should be taken out and cleaned, while soft items like herbs and petals need to be replaced when needed.

3) Feed the bag every week on the same day as it was made by using oil to regenerate its power. Use incense smoke and prayer to feed the bag whenever you need to call upon it.

4) Keep your bag dry. If it gets wet, attempt to revive its power with the Rose of Jericho plant, aka the resurrection plant.

5) There is no reason to replace your bag after a year if it's still working for you. Time and strength can differ, and different bags work better than others. Only you will know when to make a new bag and dispose of your old one.

6) When you decide to replace your bag, treat it with respect and bury it with care. This manifestation tool has been good to you, and you need to acknowledge that.

Storing Your Mojo Bags

After the first week, store your bag carefully so it will work correctly. Choose a hardwood box that is decorative and well-sealed. Place your bag inside and choose a candle to sit on the lid. Light the candle and burn it until the wax reaches the bottom of the box. This will form a sacred seal that will protect your bag until you need it.

This method should be used if you can't access your bag to feed and re-energize it regularly. For instance, if you have a jinxing bag, just in case, but you recognize the fact that you probably won't use it, you can store it in a box for a long time. Most hoodoo followers carry their positive mojo bags with them regularly, but they leave the more negative bags in storage.

Your mojo bag can be customized to suit any need. If you are looking for a new job, you can use a green bag filled with gravel root and magnetizing salt to draw well-paid employment into your life. If you are unfortunate enough to be falsely accused of a crime, then a blend of sage, galangal (aka court case root), and other herbs will help you get your case across in court. Use your mojo bag to confuse the opposition and get the judge or jury to rule in your favor.

If you prefer to buy commercial mojo bags, know the terms "double strength" or "triple strength." Ideally, this will mean the bag contains curios that are less readily available, like a human bone or a snake rib, but sometimes it just means there are more than the normal amount of items inside. Commercial bags do work, but you empower them with your essence and spirit when you make them yourself. Hoodoo is a powerful way to protect yourself, and commercial bags are less personal but can still be effective.

Chapter 6: Begin Your Conjure Work

What is Conjure Work?

An amalgam of cultural influences is involved in conjure work. The African beliefs and the Protestant base have been combined with Germanic and East European cultural influences with traditional herbal lore and knowledge that stems from the Native American community; all melded together to form Hoodoo conjure work.

It is essential to understand that conjure work is not a stand-alone practice but is merely a spiritual paradigm that lies within the more established form of folk magic that is Hoodoo. Some may call the practices listed below rootwork or spell casting but conjure work focuses more on the bastion of traditional learning.

There are two forms of conjure work based on learning and wisdom. The first stream is based on traditional practices and wisdom passed down through generations. This can be as simple as why nobody should touch your mojo bag to spiritual workings involving powders and other magical tools.

The more formal stream of conjuring involves studying intellectual streams of magic. The conjure doctors traditionally educated themselves by studying the magical arts from texts that contained spiritual and magical knowledge from all the different cultures that Hoodoo embraces. These were in the form of grimoires and other texts containing the magic of the Ancients.

The practice of conjure work has many influences and is passed from family members to their descendants. It can change and grow with every generation and develop new branches of work. What remains constant is the source of power. The natural world is filled with innate magic sources that conjure uses to influence change in people, circumstances, and fates. Conjuring involves combining these powerful ingredients to create a potent force used to manifest their desires.

Conjuring involves various implements, and we will discuss the power of candles and rootwork in later chapters. This chapter focuses on the power that can be created by combining natural elements to form powders, salves, and oils that should be readily available to Hoodoo practitioners.

When Should You Perform Your Conjuring?

Quite simply, whenever you need to. There are no hard and fast rules regarding timing or any other aspect of Hoodoo. Do them in your own time and be governed by your needs and desires. However, the power of the moon can enhance your work and give it a little oomph!

The Full Moon and Wasting

Often seen as a time of abundance, the full moon is also a final chapter of growth. As it wanes, it gets smaller and fades into darkness. If you have something or someone in your life that needs to be diminished and banished, then perform the following ritual to dispel them from your life.

Step One: Write down the name of the thing or person you want to remove from your life.

Step Two: Slice a hole into a fresh lemon and place the paper into the fruit.

Step Three: Cover the top of the paper with a piece of red pepper.

Step Four: Sew the hole with black thread.

Step Five: Pray to your favorite deity or saint to free you from the thing or person before the new moon. Mention the new moon as you don't want the negativity to return as the moon waxes.

Step Six: For the next fifteen days, repeat your prayer and watch for signs of the removal of your intention. There may be signs put in your path as the new moon begins to reappear. For instance, if you are attempting to stop smoking, then a sign or advertisement for cut-price vapes may appear. Hoodoo is telling you it recognizes what you need and is creating a path for success. You simply must become aware and take the path it shows you.

Charging Your Lucky Talisman with the Power of the Full Moon

Normally Hoodoo doesn't rely on the moon to increase the power of the ingredients it uses. They are powerful enough and only need to be cleansed with salt to recharge their energies. The moon is used to increase the spirituality of mojo bags or personal lucky charms. Letting them charge in the new moon is considered an immensely personal experience and is not for sharing with others.

The moon is used as a timepiece for conjuring. It signals when the time is right for the rituals and how to make use of its energy. Because we are human, we are affected by the moon's power, and it makes us stronger. When conjuring, the power doesn't come from the moon. It comes from us.

The Power of Powders

Every good conjuror has a stock of powerful powders to use in their work. They can be used in different forms of magic, including powering mojo bags, dressing wallets, powering love potions, casting people from your life, or attracting love. They are used to remove jinxes and bring luck, success, and wealth in different situations. Some powders are specifically mixed for job interviews or court cases, while most are more generic.

Here are just a few examples of powders all good Hoodoo conjurors need:

Aphrodite Powder

The best time to conjure is during the new moon

Ingredients

- Dried apple skins
- Pomegranate seeds
- Organic cocoa powder
- Dried mango skin
- Hibiscus petals
- Rose petals
- Hibiscus tea leaves
- Chamomile tea leaves
- Drops of passionflower essential oil

Grind all the dry ingredients together in a pestle and mortar until it's a fine powder. Add the essential oil and store it in a glass bottle.

The Wild West Powder Used to Banish or Cross

The best time to conjure is during the waning moon

Ingredients

- 3 black cloves

- Ground black pepper
- Onion powder
- Red cayenne powder
- Cumin seeds
- Fresh paprika
- Red hot chili oil

Use a small blender to mix the ingredients or grind by hand. Store in a suitable sealed container, and make sure you wash your hands when you handle this powder.

Removing the Jinx Powder

Best conjured during a waning moon

Ingredients

- Fresh mint leaves
- Dried wintergreen leaves
- Chamomile tea leaves
- Citric essential oil

Grind the ingredients together to form a paste and add to a base ingredient like cornstarch or rice flour.

Algiers Powder

Use this powder to dust the body and attract love and romance.

Best conjured during a full moon

Ingredients

- Deadnettle leaves
- Orris root
- Dried rose petals
- Vanilla essential oil

Grind and add to base flour to create dust.

Dream Powder

Use when you feel the need to have prophetic dreams and connect to the spirits as you sleep.

Best conjured during a waxing moon

Ingredients

- Licorice tea leaves
- Cinnamon powder
- Coriander seeds
- Cardamom seeds
- Ginger

Grind and add to base flour. Sprinkle onto sheets and pillowcases before sleep.

Controlling Powder

Use this powder to gain control over others. This can be in relationships or at work.

Ingredients

- Dried saltpeter
- Magnetic sand
- Myrrh
- Epsom salts

Mix the ingredients and add to base flour.

Hard Cash Powder

The best time to conjure is when the full moon occurs on Thursday, and the number 7 or 9 is part of the date.

Use his potent powder to attract wealth and money. It can be used to improve chances when gambling.

Ingredients

- Dried leaves from potentilla plant
- Chamomile tea leaves
- Cloves
- Fresh ginger
- Dried nutmeg
- A four-leaf clover
- Fresh mint
- Lavender essential oil

Grind the ingredients and store them in a glass bottle.

Cascarilla Powder

This is a simple to make powerful powder. It can be used to create a circle of protection, or it can be added to a bath to draw negativity out. Added to a floor wash, it can cleanse your house and protect your home.

The only ingredients are eggshells. Clean them and let them dry out before grinding them to a fine powder. The result is white cascarilla powder.

To make brown cascarilla powder, simply toast the eggshells in the oven until they turn brown. Then grind them until they form a fine powder.

Powders are an essential part of conjuring, as are oils. Use these recipes to make your carrier oils that can be combined with your powders or used alone to create powerful intentions.

Oils

Confusion Oil

Use this oil to make your enemies and adversaries fight each other instead of you.

Ingredients

- 1 equal part chili pepper oil
- 1 equal part patchouli oil

Add to the oil mixture

- Grains of paradise
- Blackened peppers (red, green, chili, or bell)
- Seeds from a poppy
- Mustard seeds

Adding dried vitamin E will give your oil more potency.

Conjure Oil

This all-purpose oil is used to bring more power to your conjuring work. Use it to enhance your experiences and manifest your greatest wishes.

Ingredients

- Equal parts Frankincense
- Equal parts Sandalwood
- Equal parts lotus scented oil

Mix and store in a glass bottle.

Good Luck Oil

Create a base carrier oil from jojoba oil and add the following ingredients

- 3 drops of cinnamon oil
- 20 drops of gaultheria oil

- 15 drops of essential lavender oil

If you want the oil to be more money orientated, add ginger and vetiver oil to make the intent specific to wealth.

Van Van Oil

One of the classic oils of early Hoodoo, this recipe has been passed down for generations. Some ingredients may be unobtainable, but the absence of Asian oils won't hurt the potency. This recipe is focused on the lemongrass and citronella components which you can add to create your own floral bouquet.

Ingredients

- 32 drops of citronella oil
- 16 drops lemongrass oil
- 2 drops of palmarosa oil

This is your stock oil and is a powerful base to which you can add your personal favorites. Dried herbs and essential oils will tailor your oil to suit your purpose. When using van van oil, always dilute the solution with a clean carrier oil like natural almond oil.

Other Types of Conjuring

Most practitioners recognize modern medicine and don't profess to know better than health workers and traditional doctors. They know for certain conditions, natural substances work just as well, if not better, as medical treatments.

Traditional Headache Salve

Ingredients

- 1 cup of light organic oil, sunflower, or sesame oil work great
- White sage
- Eucalyptus
- Lavender

- ½ oz pure beeswax
- Vitamin E in a liquid form
- Material for straining

All the herbs mentioned in the recipe can be fresh or dried, and the amount you add is a personal choice. Try an ounce of each and add extra if needed.

1) Now, add all the herbs to a glass casserole dish and cover with the oil.

2) Bake in an oven for 3 hours at 180 degrees.

3) Remove from the oven and let it cool for 30 minutes.

4) Use the straining cloth to remove the herbs while squeezing all the excess liquid from the cloth.

5) Put the herbal infused oil in a stainless-steel cooking pot and simmer the liquid on a low flame for 10 minutes as you add the vitamin E-liquid.

6) Add the beeswax to the oil and continue to heat until the liquid is melted and mixed.

7) Remove the cooking pot and let it rest for 5 minutes.

8) Before the mixture sets, decant it into cosmetic jars before leaving it to set.

9) Once the salve mixture has cooled and thickened, put lids on the jars.

10) Use a smudge of the salve to relieve headaches by spreading it on your temples or forehead instead of using painkillers.

Wasps Nest Conjuring

If you are lucky enough to find a dead wasp's nest in your garden, don't throw it away. Grind the nest and any accompanying dead wasps and incorporate the powder into your banishing and hex powders.

Traditionally Hoodoo believers believed wasps nests contained powerful protective powers and the teachings of Treemonisha call the phenomenon a *dirt dauber nest*. It was believed that the wasp's nest was a bringer of luck, and it kept the evil spirits away.

Mix some of your ground wasps' nest with warm water and goofer dust to form a protective mix. To create a mixture that allows you to infiltrate another person's life, a dried wasp nest is an essential ingredient. In the natural world, wasps enter a beehive by camouflaging their smell and destroy it from the inside. If this is your intention, you can use this powerful ingredient to seek retribution from within.

How to Enhance Your Conjure Work with Psalm Recitations

All forms of spiritual workers understand the power of speech. The spoken word enhances and reinforces the power of intentions. Prayers and Holy Scriptures are the most powerful forms of this type of incantation as they bring strength and reassurance to the spirit.

This is especially important in Hoodoo works as the bible is packed full of useful information that corresponds with the practice's values. It shows us how to cleanse the soul and protect the body and home from evil.

Various Important Psalms Used to Enhance Conjure Work

Psalm 51 is used to cleanse and is often used in conjunction with healing baths. It contains powerful incantations that ask for the release of iniquities and the washing away of sins. The psalm refers to original sin and the desire to seek inner truths and become purged.

The intention cast by the psalm is strongly based on being taken into the presence of the Holy Spirit and turning away from sin. Use this psalm if you feel the need to seek salvation or restore your faith and free spirit.

Psalm 64 is used for protection. Recite it when you feel under threat or want to confront your adversaries. If you need to target a person causing you harm, write down their name on a piece of brown paper, write the psalm on a white piece of paper and burn a black candle on top of the two pieces of paper.

The psalm appeals to God to protect us from evil people who use their bitter words and forked tongues to spread evil intentions. It tells of the righteous people working with God to banish all wrongdoers and make them flee from sight.

Psalm 78 mirrors Hoodoo's beliefs perfectly. It should be recited when you need to enhance your psychic abilities or charge your talisman. Pass the magic objects from one hand to another as you recite the psalm to imbue the power of your ancestors into your conjure work.

The psalm encourages us to pass on our powers and learn from those who have passed before us. It is a powerful call to believers to talk openly about their spiritual and ancient wonders.

Psalm 29 is a cleansing psalm used to protect property rather than personal items. In the psalm, images of the Lord struck the land with lightning forks describe how God cleansed the desert and stripped back the forests of Earth. Use this psalm to deep cleanse your home and strip it of all negative energy.

Psalm 65 is the gambler's psalm. If you need extra luck or are about to gamble on a project psalm, 65 is perfect for amplifying your intentions. It describes the godly actions that take place on Earth and how we are lucky to be blessed with such abundance. The psalm should be recited when creating oils and powders for luck, success, and wealth.

Most of all, your conjuring work should incorporate both streams of work. Study scientific methods alongside your ancient grimoires to create eclectic knowledge. Call upon your guardians and ancestors to assist you in your work but don't exclude modern methods and practices. Hoodoo is a perfect mix of the traditional arts and modern components.

Chapter 7: Candle Magic

Candles have been around for millenniums and were first attributed to the ancient Egyptians and some European cultures where remains of candles and their holders were found in prominent ruins. The Romans also favored the use of candles in their ceremonies, and the tradition passed to other important religions. Buddhists and other monotheistic religions used animal fat to coat reeds and form the basic concept we know today as candles.

Despite the depiction of early Hoodoo workers using candles for their working practices, the reality is that they were unavailable to early slaves, as they didn't have access to them. Candles were costly and only used in big houses, while slave quarters were lit by grease lamps or Betty lamps, as they were known, that used household fats to provide light.

Following their Emancipation, former slaves began to travel to more urban landscapes rather than staying in rural communities. Once they formed their community's outsiders recognized a way to market candles as a key part of Hoodoo rootwork and conjuring. Shops began to appear that specialized in producing candles known as "Bend over," "Easy money," and "Swift luck" to appeal to the intentions of more traditional Hoodoo roots.

A series of booklets explaining the powerful effects of candle magic was published in the 1940s and encouraged using different types of candles and how to amalgamate their use into more traditional rituals and workings already popular with Hoodoo believers.

Today candle magic appeals to beginners for much the same reasons as it did post WW2. They are an inexpensive way to start your journey. They can be found in many forms and colors and are easily accessible. Ever since Hoodoo accepted the power of candle magic, it has also explored how different magical traditions use them and adopt their beliefs. Hoodoo is always adapting and embracing new magic, and candle magic is no exception.

The Meaning of Color in Hoodoo Candle Magic

Traditionally hoodoo workers didn't believe the color of a candle was important. They mainly worked with black and white candles as they represented the good and evil aspects of life. However, as modern Hoodoo evolves, it continues to embrace other traditional beliefs and make it part of traditional conjuring and work.

Other cultures believe the color of the candle creates vibrations and spiritual connections, but that isn't the case in Hoodoo. The magic comes from the intent and not vibrations, so why would the color of a candle be important? Many Hoodoo practitioners use colored candles to remind themselves of their intent and avoid becoming distracted. Use the colors listed below to remind you why you are performing your work and refocus your efforts. Purchase long-lasting candles to allow you to perform your magic for days rather than hours, and your intent will grow over time.

Color of Candles and Their Meanings

- White candles are used for blessings and healings. They were the original candles and represented more traditional Hoodoo beliefs.

- Black candles are used to place a hex or protect individuals.

- Red candles represent blood. The liquid of life is a powerful force and so are red candles. They form the intentions regarding love and attraction and represent boldness and audacity.

- Pink candles are used to concentrate intentions on domestic affairs. They represent togetherness and respect between family members. Pink candles are used to heal a wounded spirit and regenerate positive energies in the soul.

- Orange candles are used to create doorways and remove blockages. They create a path for success and improve mental clarity and strong intentions.

- Gold candles are burned to bring wealth and fortune.

- Yellow candles signify fortune and change. They are used to create situations that can change the workers' life; this may be in relationships or practical life.

- Green candles signify material gain. They aid magic directed toward business matters and financial gain.

- Blue candles are burned for joyful magic. They signify harmony and peace and are used to bring peace to troubled households.

- Purple candles represent mastery. To cast an intention that gives you control over others, enhance your magic by burning a purple candle.

• Silver/Gray candles are helpful when casting spells for protection. They are burned to help relieve the pain and anguish connected to grief and loss.

• Brown candles are burned to ensure success regarding legal matters. This type of magic is used for court cases and reading wills.

Hoodoo Candle Terminology

Sometimes terms used within any practice don't make sense. Candle magic is no different. You will come across certain words that are important but not self-explanatory so, here's a list of words with their meanings used in candle magic:

• **Dressed Candles**: When practitioners dress candles, they use ingredients to guide the spirits to their intentions. Generally, you would choose a candle that signals your intent and then apply oil or roots to strengthen your magic. For instance, if you need to attract protection, you would choose a gray candle and apply suitable protective oil. You can use a mixture of oils to strengthen your candle by applying Fast luck oil to attract luck and protection.

A Quick Tip: Don't overload your candle with oil, or it may set on fire! Four to five drops are sufficient to dress a standard candle, and adding extra won't make your magic stronger and can cause excessive smoke.

• **Fixed Candles**: These types of candles are like dressed candles but are prepared by other people. They have been loaded with oils and herbs following intense prayers and loaded intent. They are available commercially and are sold in containers with printed instructions for use.

• **Loaded Candles**: When a candle has been carved into or hollowed out and then filled with oils, roots, or herbs, it is called a "loaded candle." You can load your own and tailor your candle to suit your intention, or you can buy pre-prepared candles from specialist suppliers. If doing a homemade candle, remember to choose a chunky candle as tapered ones will split and crack.

• **Carved Candles:** Carving a name or symbol into a candle is used to direct magic to a specific person or thing. Carving someone's name directs the intention of your magic towards them or makes it work for them. More generic symbols represent how you want your magic to work. For instance, the carving of an eye into a candle signifies protection.

• **Rolled Candles:** Candles rolled in oil and herbs are called "rolled candles" and can look impressive. There are some dangers when using these types of candles, as the herbs will affect how the candle burns. Exterior materials will fall off and can cause fire and smoke to appear.

All candles are potential fire hazards and should always be watched. Encased candles are safer than traditional ones and are less likely to cause damage. Holders and cases are a great way to minimize the dangers and make your magic work safe.

Hoodoo Figure Candles

Just like colored candles, effigy or form candles aren't part of traditional Hoodoo works. They are a relatively new concept and aren't meant to represent human figures or spirits. They are used to remind you of your intent and help you refocus your efforts.

Novelty-shaped candles are a cause of debate among Hoodoo believers. Certain people feel they bring the practice into disrepute and are tacky and powerless. Others believe that the physical representation greatly enhances the magic rituals. Another sticking point is what the symbols represent. Some people look at a figure and see one meaning, while others will see a contradictory representation.

As a Hoodoo candle magic practitioner, the best way to decide is to look at the shaped candle and decide what it means to you.

- **Skull Candles**: These represent the mind and are used to penetrate thoughts and redirect how you want someone to act. The color of the skull is causally related to the intention you want to set, and white skulls are particularly effective for mourning and easing grief. Skulls are also used to incite lust and passion in someone you want to attract.

- **Devil or Satan Candles:** Placed in doorways and windows, these candles will help banish evil spirits and prevent them from entering the home. Red devils are associated with base emotions like lust and passion, and their presence will spice up any rituals involving sexual intent.

- **Baphomet Sabbatical Goat**: Used to coerce others in matters that aren't sexual, the goat represents power and force. Burn these candles when you wish to dominate the thoughts of others and make them do tour bidding.

- **Cat-Shaped Candles:** Traditionally associated with luck and good fortune, burn these candles when you need your luck to turn.

- **Seven Knob Candles**: A powerful candle with seven indentations, this candle is meant to burn over seven days. You can use it to wish for one thing for seven days, or you can wish for seven different things.

- **Marriage or Lovers Candle**: The image of a loving couple in an embrace is burned to enhance love and unions. There are also separated couples which show two people back-to-back. Burn these to encourage kinder divorces or separations.

- **Money Pyramid Candle**: Often decorated with an all-seeing eye, these candles represent power and wealth. The symbolic eye will help protect your possessions and home from theft and damage.

- Witch candles are burned to represent the power of magic and energy.

Multipurpose candles on the market can represent all forms of power. The image of male and female genitalia or more traditional satanic forms can be purchased, but it doesn't mean they should be!

Double action candles do exactly what their name suggests. They provide the user with the power to reverse situations and are larger than the standard candle. One half of the candle is black, and the other half is colored to fit with your intention.

Red and black candles are burned to stop someone or something from destroying your life.

White and black candles provide a powerful original combination of the original colors. Burn these to remove a bad hex or jinx that has been applied to you or your household.

Green and black candles will help reverse your financial misfortunes.

Triple action candles are made with sections in red, white, and green and represent a time when you need help for most things in your life. They will attract love, dispel negativity and evil while drawing wealth and good luck to you.

How to Read Candle Burning

Interpreting what the flame of a candle means is subjective. It can change depending on the material used in the candle and what the wick is made from. If you plan on mastering the art of candle readings, make sure you buy your candle from the same source, so the flame they provide is consistent. To become a master candle conjurer, you should make your candles to know exactly what you are getting.

Always remember that Hoodoo is guiding you to the outcome it believes you deserve. If you choose a badly made candle and receive a message that sends you down a different path, then maybe it was meant to be. Signs and interpretation will become second nature to you as your work improves, and you will learn to read them and understand the magical meaning behind them.

Candle Flames and What They Mean

There is a myriad way a candle can burn, and they all mean different things. When you burn your magic candles, make sure the flame can burn true and isn't affected by drafts and other exterior influences.

- Steady upward flame means all is going well.
- Jumping flame means that someone is desperate to contact you. The spirits are telling you something, and only you will know what. This flame isn't necessarily negative as it can mean the spirits are showing their encouragement for your work.
- Dancing flame. When the flame is flickering from side to side rhythmically, it indicates that your energies are chaotic. It tells you to take a minute and refocus. You have the power required for successful working, but it has been distracted.
- Shrinking flame means a lack of energy. If you see this sign, it means you may take longer than expected to reach your goal.
- Heightened flame has mixed messages for you. Your work will be completed faster than you thought, but it also indicates the results may be short-lived.
- Blue flames normally are seen at the base of the wick. They mean you are on the right track and are an indication your magic will succeed.

- Green flames mean wealth. This isn't always financially important; it just means that whatever you wish for will come in abundance.

- White smoke is a positive sign from the spirits and means you are working successfully.

- Black smoke is a signal you are being worked against. You need to leave the work and cast a road opener or blockage destroying spell before you recommence with this intention.

- Noises accompanying your flame are a sure sign the spirits are trying to communicate with you. Any popping, hissing, or crackling that isn't associated with the natural burning process will alert you to their presence.

How to Read the Wax When Your Candle is Burning

This type of divination is known as ceromancy and is performed by interpreting how wax runs down a free-standing candle.

Reading the wax and how it melts is a great way to determine how your workings are progressing. If your candle is properly contained and on a level surface the readings, will be more accurate. Here are some ways to interpret the wax from your candle:

- **Tears:** If the wax looks like human tears, it indicates that tears will be shed because of your work. If they stop before the candle runs out, then the grief will be short-lived and temporary.

- **Pinnacles:** If the wax runs down the candle but doesn't reach the bottom or break off, this means that someone involved in the spells is holding on to the past. They may have grievances or issues that mean they are tainted, and your workings won't succeed.

- No wax drips indicate the highest level of success. Your workings have been perfectly executed, and you are guaranteed success.

- If the candle opens like a flower and spreads wax into an uneven puddle, it is a sign your wish has been granted, but it suggests there are other paths to be taken. Your work is far from finished, and you need to concentrate on other areas of your life.

- Wax down one side means something is off-kilter. Your spell is going to be incomplete, and you may have a spiritual imbalance.

How to Read the Wax Puddles Once the Candle Has Burned

The wax should form a recognizable shape when performing certain rituals. Heart-shaped puddles for love and flat smooth puddles when performing more neutral spells are normal, but some shapes can indicate the presence of negativity.

- Claw-like wax remnants mean someone is spreading malicious rumors and gossip about you. Repeat your work until the wax burns smoothly.

- Wax puddles that look like genitalia can indicate infidelity and troubled relationships.

- Pillars that look unnatural or monster-like show the spell has been unsuccessful due to outside turbulence. Cast powder or oil to remove these influences.

- Coffin-shaped puddles mean that your hex or jinx spells worked, and the threat against you is defeated.

Chapter 8: The Craft of Rootwork

During the era of slavery, control was stripped from slaves' lives. They had little or no control over how they lived. While their masters may have retained control of their bodies, they had no say in how the slaves retained their spirits. Their imagination and the gift of stories meant they could keep their spirits up even during the most harrowing times.

There are multiple stories about men from Africa called John or Jack who inspired the slaves with stories of their deeds and how they got one over on their masters. Perhaps the most famous is High John, the conqueror and a huge man who hated being a slave. His trickery and skill at avoiding work made him one of the most celebrated figures in African folklore.

High John the Conqueror

Some say that High John was an African prince sold into slavery, while other tales tell of a commoner. His trickery and ability to avoid work were legendary. His strength and luck ensured that every bet he laid was successful, and although he played dumb, he always outsmarted those who opposed him. He was associated with the Ipomea Jalapa, known as the most powerful root in a Hoodoo worker's bag of tricks.

Most practitioners always carry High John Root with them to remove obstacles and conquer their enemies. It magnifies the root's lucky element when it's stored in a green mojo bag, and it will help attract money and wealth to the carrier. Use the chips from the root to enhance cooking and use them in oils to dress your salads.

Other Popular Roots and Herbs Used in Hoodoo and Their Magical Properties

Angelica Root

Also known as Archangel root, sprinkle dried angelica in the four corners of your home to protect it and ward off evil. Use the root to enhance any workings aimed at purification and uncrossing hexes. Angelica will also help bring back lost loves and reignite passions.

Bats Head Root

Also known as Devil pod, horny bulls head, and ling nut, this strange-looking black root appears just like the head of a devil. Use it when you want your wishes to come true and remove those that stand in your way.

Blood Rot Root

Use this root for multiple results. It helps resolve marital and family disputes while improving your sex life. Burning the root during a ritual will stop someone else from taking your lover, while placing it in the window will attract new partners. Blood rot root is a popular ingredient for marriage-based rootwork.

Calamus Root

This root should be burned while performing other works to strengthen the potency of the original spell. It is a dominating root and adds strength to any situation.

Devils Shoestring Root

Use this to change your luck at work or attract a new job. Carry it in your pocket when seeking employment or attending interviews. This root will also help you gain control over the opposite sex.

Fennel

Hang fennel in your home and workplace to protect you from negative energies and spirits. It is especially effective for women and can attract money and wealth for females.

Hazel

It is used to make amulets for fertility that are traditionally given to new brides as a gift. Hang hazel twigs from windows to ward off lightning strikes.

Lavender

This herb is used to bring harmony and mutual sexual satisfaction to couples experiencing problems in the bedroom. Some Hoodoo rootworkers use it to stop cruel partners from abusing their spouses by rubbing it on the victim as a shield.

Magnolia

Males use buds from this herbal flower to attract female attention. It is also used to elicit fidelity and stop partners from straying.

Nutmeg

This lucky herb is a favorite for gamblers. It attracts wealth and luck, so it is regarded as a sign of prosperity.

Galangal Root

Known as Chewing John root, this is a powerful protection root. Chew it in your mouth while casting reverse hex spells and then spit the remains out to dispel them from your life. If you face a court case, burn this root two weeks before the court date for guaranteed success. When used to attract wealth, wrap money around the root, and it will multiply threefold.

Ginger

Most people who know about healthy eating know the benefits of ginger. Hoodoo is no different, and ginger is one of the most versatile roots used in rootwork. It is used to promote sensuality, self-confidence, and prosperity. Use it to speed up your rootwork and add an extra dose of potency. If you can source a ginger root that resembles the human form, you can perform powerful magic, and cast commanding spells with ease.

Queen Elizabeth Root

Also known as orris root, this is especially influential when used in rootwork and conjuring for love and sex. It attracts the opposite sex while increasing the potential for long time love. It is used in spells to strengthen marriage and increase fertility. Sprinkle it on sheets for some passionate nights filled with love and great sex.

Hyssop

This cleansing herb is sourced from Southern Europe and is part of the mint family. Its benefits have been known to herbal practitioners as far back as Biblical times. In Hoodoo, it is a forceful herb when used to cleanse the home and remove hexes.

Five Finger Grass

Also known as cinquefoil, this herb is used to attract success. Bathe in water infused with five-finger grass solution for nine days to remove a stubborn curse or jinx. You can make tea with dried leaves that improve your health and wealth when drunk.

Licorice Root

Use when you need to change someone's mind or gain control of their thinking. Licorice is a powerful ingredient when used in controlling powders.

Mugwort

Also known as Artemisia vulgaris, use a solution containing this herb to clean your magical tools like crystals and talismans. It will remove negativity and restore their strength. Place it in your shoes before you go out for extra energy and a spring in your step!

Parsley

These tasty leaves are much more than a handy cooking ingredient. They are used to promote calm and peace in the household and can guard your food against any form of contamination. Parsley is used for aiding healing following serious illness or surgery and is used in spells about health and vitality. If you feel out of sorts or stuck in a rut, cast a conjure using parsley, and you will immediately feel the benefits.

Pepper Tree

It stands as a powerful form of protection, and it also has healing properties and can aid the recovery of people who have been ill or had surgery.

Thyme

If you need to boost your psychic powers or purify your rootwork, thyme will help you gain knowledge and courage to carry on. It is commonly used for grounding spells and conjuring.

Witch Hazel Bark

Here we see one of the influences that Native Americans brought to Hoodoo practitioners. It is used to heal skin conditions and can be used as a gargle to treat oral problems. When incorporated into rootwork, it reduces passion and encourages chastity in those who may need to focus on other subjects. Carrying it on your person also helps reduce grief following a death.

This list is far from comprehensive, and there are thousands more herbs and roots available. They all have slightly different properties, and you can explore them ad infinitum. Hoodoo is primarily about discovering new ways to encompass other beliefs and cultures into your personal magic, and studying how other religions and beliefs use nature is one way to expand your knowledge.

How to Create Amulets and Talismans with Your Roots and Herbs

First, let's distinguish the two terms and what the difference is between them. An amulet is a natural object that can be blessed and consecrated for use in magic and conjuring. Amulets are then charged with intention depending on the power the user requires. They can be charged with attractions and with repelling powers to keep the wearer safe and lucky.

Talismans are man-made objects charged similarly. They can be crafted from many materials and worn around the neck, as a ring, or any other way the user requires. They can be decorated with natural objects like crystals or stones, but they are made by hand, often by the rootworker who is going to charge them.

How to Make an Amulet

Choose a durable material to create your amulets, like stone or gemstones. For this example, we will use a stone known in spiritual circles as a Hag stone. This is a stone that has been naturally worn down by running water to create a hole or holes that are ascetically pleasing.

The shape of your stone may immediately suggest to you what its potential power may be. A heart-shaped rock will be ideal for love spells and rootwork, while a stone that resembles a dagger will be used for protection. Now you need to make your amulet wearable. Use cords and natural fibers to enable the wearer to use it as a necklace or bracelet.

Now your talisman needs to be consecrated and cleansed. Use water and sacred salt to remove any impurities and negativity from your amulet and let it dry naturally. Now pass the stone through the burning smoke of your preferred herbs until you feel it is ready to be charged.

Charging your amulet is a personal experience and involves you calling to your favorite deities and asking them to hear your intentions. Ask them to protect you and your amulet in times of danger and bestow their love and strength on you when you need them.

Although the talisman is a natural object, that doesn't mean you can't decorate it. Use magical symbols and vibrant paint to make your amulet decorative and increase its magical potency. Add beads and crystals to the cords you used and make your amulet a stunning piece of jewelry.

How to Make a Talisman

Choose the central object you want to be the focus of your talisman. This can be a pendant you already use or a ring. You can use coins and other metal objects like keys or decorative wirework to make your piece look beautiful. Clay and metal objects can be engraved with special symbols or sigils that can be incredibly powerful in the use of your talismans.

Determine what the purpose of your talisman is. Do you need it to attract love, or is it a more protective charm? You can use the lunar cycles to enhance your talisman's strength by choosing the best time of the month to create your piece. Use leather straps to make your talisman wearable, as leather represents an amalgam of the natural and man-made world.

Use your herbs and roots to create a potion or infusion to bless your talisman. Sprinkle it with a few drops daily, and make sure you keep your talisman in a safe place. Now charge your talisman with your inner energy. Allow the strength of your intentions to wash over the piece until it vibrates with your spirit. Summon your favorite spirits and deities and ask for their blessing and protection in all your works.

If you have any excess energy in your physical body, cast a simple grounding spell like the one below:

Burn sage and sandalwood on a slate disc and light a white candle that sits on top of a natural stone. Seat yourself in a comfortable position and connect to the flame your candle is creating. Stare at it as it dances and breathe deeply as you watch.

Now visualize roots growing from your arms and legs. Imagine them burrowing into the ground and revel in your connection with the earth and the universe. Now use these roots to channel all the anxieties and fears you have ever felt and feel them disappear into the ground. Focus on your breath as you feel your excess energies and negativity drain away.

Grounding yourself is not just about getting rid of anxiety and feeling chilled. It is all part of your spiritual connection to the very fabric of the cosmos and the power it holds. Let the candle burn for an hour after you have completed the grounding, so it infuses into every fiber of your being. Once the candle has burned down, the stone it was sitting on can be used as a natural amulet.

Although there are no hard and fast rules regarding the use of these objects, most people find that talismans are more effective for attraction and projections, while amulets are used for protection and repelling.

How to Use Magic Herbs and Roots in Your Spell Work

1) Rolling your candles in dried herbs and roots will help your candle burn more effectively.

2) Burn dried herbs or roots on charcoal or slate disks

3) Use as incense

4) Sturdy herbs can be burned directly. Flammable herbs include sage, rosemary, eucalyptus, and Italian cypress, but you must always take precautions

5) Use them to make tinctures so their power will continue to work for months at a time.

How to Prepare and Harvest Your Roots

Fall is the perfect time to begin your harvesting. All the vibrant energy of summer has retreated into the plants' roots that bloomed, and the goodness and nutrients are firmly ensconced within. This makes it the perfect time to harvest and prepare roots for use.

You need to respect the plants you harvest and make sure you cause no damage. Ask the plants for permission to use their bounty before you carefully take what you need.

Here is a timeframe to help you become a sustainable herb and root master

- Annual plants should be harvested once their full cycle has been completed
- Perennials shouldn't be harvested in the first three years because the active compounds they contain won't be present until they have matured

- More substantial shrubs and bushes will have prolific offshoots that allow you to harvest without disturbing the main taproot. This helps their chances of survival and growth

- The sap is affected by solar cycles, so harvest your roots in the morning or early evening when the vitality and energy is at premium levels

Cleaning Your Roots

Remove the soil and dirt gently and with care. An old toothbrush is perfect as it can remove the dirt without removing the tiny hairs that cover the roots. These hairs are packed with important constituents that need to be preserved.

Any cutting needs to be done when fresh as dry roots are difficult to cut cleanly. Once you have cut your roots to the required size, you need to dry them sympathetically. This can be done by laying the cuttings on trays, placing them outside out of direct sunlight but in a warm atmosphere. You can use a food dehydrator on a low setting of 150 degrees or a regular oven on a low setting with the door left open.

Quick Note: Some roots will attract moisture and become soft, discard any limp or flaccid roots immediately.

There are different rituals for charging your herbs and roots and preparing them for rootwork, so here is a general tutorial you can adapt for your uses

- Place your herbs and roots on a sacred surface and bless them with a prayer or psalm

- Use a smudging stick to bless the offerings

- Leave the roots and herbs outside in the light of the full moon

- Place the roots and herbs in a container filled with sacred salt

Chapter 9: The Hoodoo Divination

In the past, divination rituals were often reserved for professional sightseers and who had the gift of fortune-telling. Ordinary people would seek their help and ask them to do readings on their behalf. As the practice of Hoodoo grew, our hardworking ancestors realized that they could perform rituals, but they didn't have the means to purchase fancy accessories like tarot cards and crystals to carry out their rituals.

Household objects and other tools they had to hand were substituted for their divination rites. Ordinary cards were used instead of tarot cards, and commonly sourced objects replaced ivory in the practice of cleromancy.

Here we study how modern-day Hoodoo followers can gain an insight into what the future holds for them and others.

Cartomancy

When you play a poker game or other household games, most people don't realize they are playing with the tarot card's original form. As far back as the 14th-century, gypsies used ordinary cards to foresee the future. The four suit designs were designed to represent the four elements of earth, wind, fire, and water. Each suit then contains a hierarchy that represents the leaders and their subjects. The King and queen are served by their pages, and the rest of the cards represent the subjects who serve them. The 52 cards all have separate meanings that govern how you read a spread.

Card Spreads

This is the term used to describe how the cards are dealt and what to expect from certain combinations.

- Single cards are used for rapid answers to straightforward questions
- Three-card spreads are used to signify the past, present, and future
- Nine-card spreads are used to represent the past, present, and future with added layers of information
- The Gypsy Spider Web is a tableau of cards made up of 21 individual cards in three rows of seven to create a detailed reading of the past, present, and future.

There are myriad ways of creating card spreads and possible interpretations. The hidden nuances behind the spread will mean different things to different people. However, a basic knowledge of what the cards represent will help you get an accurate and informative reading.

The Definition and Meanings Behind the Cards

The Suits

- **Hearts:** Representing the element of fire, this suit is connected to the home and emotional affairs
- **Diamonds:** Representing the element of wind, this suit is connected to work-related affairs and other external issues
- **Clubs:** Representing the element of earth, and this suit relates to financial and money related matters
- **Spades:** Representing the element of water, and this suit is related to obstacles and roadblocks that can cause problems in your life

The Individual Cards and Their Meaning

Hearts

The regal cards of the pack are known as identifier cards and will represent a certain person in your life

- **King:** A sage man who will give excellent advice
- **Queen:** A kindly lady with light hair
- **Jack:** A younger person of indistinctive gender with blonde hair
- **Ten:** Joy and happiness
- **Nine:** Your wishes and hopes will all come true
- **Eight:** your social life will improve as you get invited to parties
- **Seven:** Broken promises and treachery
- **Six:** Serendipity and good fortune
- **Five:** Envious people surround you

- **Four:** A change of surroundings and maybe marriage later in life
- **Three:** Slow down and be cautious
- **Two:** Solidifying a relationship with engagement, success, and wealth
- **Ace:** New beginnings, love, and joy

Diamonds

- **King:** Powerful, stubborn, and obstinate man with light hair
- **Queen:** Flirtatious woman fond of partying and loves to chat about others
- **Jack:** A younger person with light hair. The black sheep of the family with a dubious past
- **Ten:** New environment. Positive changes and success
- **Nine:** Unexpected financial news, new career opportunities, change
- **Eight:** Marriage in maturity, traveling in cold environments, money changes
- **Seven:** Unexpected gifts, work-related issues
- **Six:** Issues with second marriages
- **Five:** Career success, happy family life
- **Four:** Unexpected legacies or bequests, money
- **Three:** Issues with legal matters, family disputes
- **Two:** Love affairs that aren't conventional and aren't popular, fallouts between business partners
- **Ace:** Gifts of jewelry, correspondence regarding financial matters

Clubs

- **King**: Loving man with dark hair who is magnanimous and kind
- **Queen:** Older woman with dark hair who is attractive and confident
- **Jack**: Younger friend with dark locks who is constant and reliable
- **Ten:** Surprising financial news, foreign travel, luck
- **Nine**: New romantic relationships, be more accepting and indulgent
- **Eight**: Marriage and relationship issues, others envy you
- **Seven:** Beware the opposite gender, wealth, and success
- **Six:** Seek help with money matters; you will succeed in business matters
- **Five:** New acquaintances and a happy marriage, friends who will come to your assistance
- **Four:** Bad times lie ahead, and you will encounter betrayal and dishonesty
- **Three**: Marriage to a wealthy partner, financial assistance from your spouse
- **Two:** backstabbing and lies will disappoint you
- **Ace**: Your post will contain a letter about finances, happiness, health, and wisdom

Spades

- **King**: A powerful man who is self-confident and has jet black hair
- **Queen**: A dark-haired widow who is immoral and deceitful

- **Jack:** A younger man with questionable ethics but is well-meaning and immature, dark-haired males
- **Ten:** Incarceration, bad news, bad luck, and worries
- **Nine:** Low energy, general misfortune, death and destruction, overall depression
- **Eight:** Disrupted plans, cancellations, and disputes at work and home
- **Seven:** Lost companions, friendships destroyed, possible losses
- **Six:** Small triumphs that add up to major changes
- **Five:** Outside influences will disrupt your family life; expect a reversal of fortunes
- **Four:** Times of bad health, broken pledges, financial worries
- **Three:** Infidelity and breakdown of relationships
- **Two:** Difficult decisions regarding marriage and partnership, separation and lies
- **Ace:** Death and disruption, arguments, and obsessions

Of course, some people play their card games with jokers, and cartomancy is no different. If you see a joker in your spread, it means new beginnings and taking risks.

How to Shuffle the Deck

Everyone has their own style of shuffling and cutting the deck. If someone shuffles for a short time, this means they are more likely to want an answer for specific questions right away. Those who shuffle more are interested in a broader spectrum style of reading.

Readers should ask seekers to cut the deck into multiple piles before creating the required spread. Seekers who cut shallow are reluctant to trust the advice they will be given, while a deep cut indicates confidence and belief in the reader. Shallow cutters also worry about just how much of their true nature is about to be relieved and are anxious about the reading.

Truly gifted cartomancy readers rely on a mix of knowledge of what the cards mean and their own intuition. The spread is just the start of a journey into self-discovery for both the reader and the seeker, and the more you practice, the better your results will be.

Augury

This form of divination involves reading omens and signs to foretell the future. Hoodoo is firmly rooted in the natural world, so it follows that omens and signs that occur in nature are a trusted indication of the future. The practice was recorded as far back as Ancient Egyptian times, yet the use of formal augury is thought to be Roman.

The word auspice is derived from the Latin terms *auspicium* and *auspex*, which means "looking at birds," so the original practitioners based their beliefs on birds' movement and the patterns they formed.

If you would like to learn how to perform this particular form of divination, you can seek wild birds to read. However, the most powerful first step you can take is to let the birds come to you. You can practice the art of divination in the wild, but the most significant messages will come from birds who visit you. It is a message from the divine world, after all!

What Different Types of Birds Mean

Crows and Ravens

Black birds are often connected to bad luck and death. Maybe because they are black and have strong associations with witchcraft, or maybe because black is the color of evil. Either way, modern misconceptions should be ignored when practicing augury. These birds are the harbinger of benevolent messages, and they bring protection and good luck. Crows and ravens are two of the smartest animals in the world and, as such, should be linked to positive connections with the spiritual plane.

Hawks

These types of birds represent foresightedness and the need to take notice of your surroundings. Their superior eyesight in the wild signifies your need to see things clearly and view the bigger picture with wisdom and careful consideration. Seeing a hawk should be considered a blessing.

Owls

In some cultures, owls are psychopomps. This is a creature or spirit sent to earth to guide a soul to heaven following their death. Because of these beliefs, Hoodoo augury regards the appearance of an owl as a sign someone will die. Native Americans believe evil spirits send the owl to spy on humans and perform negative tasks on Earth.

Hummingbirds

These beautiful, strong, and fast birds are a joy to behold. Their appearance means the spirits are sending you a message of joy and love. The dance they perform is nature's way of displaying what perfect balance and harmony look like and how we must strive to achieve it in our own lives.

Doves

These white birds are often seen as a sign of hope and good intentions, while others see them as symbols of death and grief. Just like all black birds aren't negative signs, all-white birds aren't positive signs.

How Many Birds Are There?

Now consider the number of birds interacting with each other. Are there two? Are there ten? Or are there too many to count? Here an understanding of numerology will help you, but it isn't essential. If you see solo birds, they are a message to individuals to recharge and refuel their psychic and physical batteries. Pairs of birds signify romance or joining, while multiple birds show the strength of belief. Augury is all about how you interpret these signs, so you may see a recurrence of your favorite number if the spirits are trying to connect.

How Are the Birds Behaving?

The bird's physical behavior is a crucial part of the process. Are they just flying, or are they behaving differently? When you study the way birds behave, you will soon pick up on any anomalies. When a storm is coming, birds will act out of character so they could be warning you of physical dangers. Are they looking for food or a mate? This could mean you are being told to get yourself out there and improve your social ties.

How to Read Birds Flight Patterns

The position of the birds is also important. Are they concentrated in the East, or are they flying south? The ancient teachings tell us that the four directions of the compass are important when reading bird augur. The cardinal directions can mean different things.

- South represents love, heat, and passion and indicates you need to pay attention to these areas
- East indicates the Garden of Eden. It signifies a place of safety and salvation where you can find security and love
- West has two differing associations. Because the sun sets in the West, it is considered a place of darkness and cold.

However, because of its association with the biblical figure Abraham, it also signifies a divine blessing and liberation from your enemies.

- North can mean permanence, or it can be read as a sign of destruction depending on your biblical leanings.

Just as these cardinal points have mixed messages, so do other aspects of augury. Dead birds would seem to represent death, but they can just mean a metaphorical death like the end of a relationship. The main point to remember is to have fun with your augury and take from it the knowledge you need and the comfort you seek.

Cleromancy

The ancient art of bone reading may seem at odds with the modern world with its use of bones as fortune-telling tools. The truth is you can use all kinds of cool stuff to perform cleromancy like dominos, stones, shells, or dice to cast your bones.

If you prefer traditional methods, then poultry bones leftover from a chicken dinner are perfect for making your tools.

How to Cure Bones

Boil some water in a large pot or your favorite cauldron and keep it on the flame. Now put your leftover bones in the pot and boil them for 20 minutes.

Once all the flesh has been stripped off, take them from the pot and let them cool down. Fill a plastic container or bucket with a mixture of ½ gallon of water plus ¼ cup of bleach. Soak the bones for an hour.

Once the bones are clean, place them in the sunlight to dry for at least a day.

Bless your bones with some sage smudging or place them in sacred salt while sprinkling anointed oil on them. Ask for divine help and appeal to your favorite deities as you work.

How to Use Your Bones

The Yes/No Method

Take a bone and ask a question. Now drop it from your hand onto your table or altar. If the bone lies in a vertical position, the answer is no, and if it's horizontal, the answer is yes.

Scrying

This is a more exacting science. Like reading tea leaves, scrying involves reading the pictorial message the bones are displaying. Take your bones and drop them onto a table or altar from a height of 12". Now consider what the bones are telling you. Just concentrate and let your mind be filled with images and ideas that appear.

The Drawstring Bag Method

Personalize your bones with images. Letters or symbols representing your creativity and energy can be combined with keywords or drawings to make your readings more intense. Ask your question as you draw bones out of a drawstring bag and apply the meanings to your dilemmas.

This type of divination is also known as sortilege. Any objects can be included in your personalized divination set, so create a sortilege kit with more personal items and fewer occult pieces. These can include feathers, pieces of driftwood, buttons, pieces of jewelry, and decorative rocks.

Most diviners will tell you that the best way to get accurate readings is to create your own set. Include unique and powerful pieces that resonate with your life. These can include commercially available items, but you shouldn't buy completed sets if you want your readings to be specific to you.

Oneiromancy

The art of divination through dreams is possibly the simplest form of connecting with the spiritual plane and the Divine. You need only to sleep and await the messages they send. They will have different meanings depending on the recipient, but some common interpretations of dream images shown below will help you decide what your dreams are telling you.

Most Common Dreams and What They Mean

1) Teeth Falling Out: Often interpreted as a signal of death, more symbolically, it represents a loss of vitality. The spirits are telling you to take care of yourself and increase your energy levels.

2) Driving: Vehicles represent our soul, and when you dream of driving, it represents the evolution of your life. If you dream you are a passenger, it could signify you need to take charge of your own decisions.

3) Flying: You are ready to make changes and advance your life. You are headed for a time of decisions and new beginnings.

4) Spiders: The fear and anxiety caused by arachnids represent an authoritative figure causing you stress. This could be an overwhelming relationship issue or a work problem.

5) Climbing a Mountain: This dream represents an inner need for knowledge. You are striving for self-improvement and advancement. The spirits are telling you to believe in yourself and climb the spiritual mountain that leads to your elevation.

Some Hoodoo rituals can prepare you for clearer dreams and signify you are ready to receive your messages from the spirits. Use candles, incense, and herbal tea to create a calming atmosphere before you go to sleep. Leave offerings to the deities and spirits on your nightstand to encourage them to communicate via dreams.

The moon and other elements will help you enhance the rituals and make them successful. Morpheus is the ultimate god of sleep and dreams, but you can call upon any deity you like. Hypnos, Diana, Chandra, and Ira are all symbolic figures from different cultures.

Chapter 10: Hoodoo Spells for Love and Attraction

As the song tells us, "Love is all you need," and most of us hope and pray that our romantic relationships and attachments are successful and happy. In the real world, we know that love and passion are often the catalysts for some of the most destructive emotions and actions we will be subject to. Love binds us to people, and even when threatened, we will fight for our love and resort to all methods to keep it in our lives.

Our relationships are often the basis of how we live, and most couples know they need work. Wise pairings will work together to resolve issues and treat each other with respect. Outside influences will always affect relationships with families interfering and other parties trying to create problems. Jealousy and losing trust are often the key factors that cause strife and difficulties, even for the most loved couples.

Love spells may seem like the perfect way to strengthen bonds and restore the affection and love that may have been lost. Casting spells and conjures offers solutions to problems and can seem like the last alternative for failing relationships.

The truth is that if a relationship is failing, it may be for the right reasons, and no amount of Hoodoo or other interference will save it. One person may be ready to quit and leave to look for love elsewhere, while another may feel like the love is worth saving. In situations like this, then no spell or potion will work to keep them together. You can only influence and strengthen true emotions, and if the attraction isn't there, then the spell won't work.

How to Cast Spells for You and Your Partner

If you are experiencing difficulties, but you still feel you can save your relationship, then a soul mate spell will help you come together again. Have a full and frank discussion where you both air your views before you undertake any Hoodoo rituals so you can both benefit from the power of the magic.

Create a Safe Space

Ensure that both of you are in a good space, mentally and physically. If you are surrounded by positive energy, you will be more receptive to the spell and less likely to suffer any harm.

Now create a safe space to cast your spell. Form a circle of protection using herbs, sacred salt, and crystals and enter it when you feel ready. Breathe deeply and use prayers and recitations to make your space feel special.

There are several deities associated with love and passion; you can choose your favorite from the following:

- Aphrodite, the Greek goddess of love
- Cernunnos, the Celtic horned god of passion
- Dionysus, the Greek god of fertility, winemaking, insanity, and madness
- Ishtar, the Mesopotamian goddess of sexual love

- Ptah, the Egyptian goddess of fertility and love
- Odin, the Norse god of fertility and strength
- Krishna, the Hindu god of compassion, tenderness, and love

Choose your spell carefully and be aware it comes with consequences. Do your research and consult with expert practitioners to choose the spell you need. Follow the instructions carefully and establish what the different outcomes will be. White magic is a more successful path to choose when casting romance spells, but sometimes the darker magic works better when banishing lovers or getting rid of your competition.

Examples of Available Spells and How to Perform Them

Quick Conciliation Spell

This is used to bring partners back together following an argument or separation period because of a disagreement.

What You Need

- Handwritten psalm 32
- Pink tapered candle
- 8 tacks
- Jar of honey
- Apiece of slate to burn the candle on
- Pin or needle

Take the paper you have written the psalm on and turn it over. Now write the name of the person you argued with on the paper.

Take the pin or needle and carve the name of your loved one into the candle three times.

Stand the candle on the piece of slate and surround the base with the tacks.

Cover the tacks with spoons of honey to sweeten the pain caused by your argument.

Burn the candle for three consecutive days while reciting Psalm 32. After the third day, your spell is cast.

Honey Jar Spell

If you feel your relationship has become staid or boring and you want to restore the love and romance (not the lust, that's a whole different spell!) to your life, then try this spell.

What You Need

- Pen and paper
- Slate to place your candle on
- Pink or red candles
- Your preferred love herbs and roots like cloves, rose petals, cardamom, and magnolia
- Attraction oil or powder
- Jar with honey in it

Honey is often used to attract other people because that is its natural state. Bees are drawn to honey and nectar, and so it will attract love. In ancient days honey was also used as offerings to love and fertility deities to access their gifts.

Take the piece of paper and write the name of the person you want to reconnect to three times. Now rotate the paper and write your name three times, so it overlaps their name and forms a block. Circle the block with loving words and phrases like "love me" and "come back to me" without lifting your pen from the paper.

Now add the oils and herbs to the paper. You can add some personal items to strengthen your honey and infuse it with your intentions. Use hair from your heads or even bodily fluids (use your imagination here) to enhance the mix. All these items should be kept in the center of the paper.

Now charge the jar with herbs, roots, and other items related to loving. Rosemary represents fidelity, while orange peel signifies joy. Use your favorite ingredients to charge the honey before you add the paper.

Now place the paper into the honey jar while reciting the following words *"This honey is sweet to me just like (say the name of the person you are influencing) will be sweet and loving to me."*

Lick any excess honey from your hands and repeat the ritual a further two times. Close the lid of the jar and place it in a cool place. Your honey jar of love is now complete and ready for use.

Place your candle on the slate and use the honey from the jar to anoint it. Light the candle and ask for help from the spirits and deities of love. Repeat for three days, and the spell will be cast.

Dragons Blood Resin Love Spell

While the name sounds quite dark, this spell is performed using natural ingredients to make your former lover aware that you still love them and compel them to return. It will work to make them return and give your relationship another chance at working.

What You Need

- Embers for burning
- Copper dish
- Dragon's blood resin or essential oil (Dragon's blood is a natural product obtained from tropical plants and sold by specialist Hoodoo stores)

Perform this ritual when the moon is turning from new to full. Whenever possible, this should be on Friday at midnight. Take the embers from a fire and place them in the copper bowl. Sprinkle your oil or resin over the embers and recite the following incantation:

"This dragon's blood is mine to burn just as my lovers' heart is mine to turn. May they have no pleasure or rest until they return to my loving arms. This is how it should be, and so it will be"

The spell is now cast.

How to Get Rid of an Unwanted Lover

This spell is effective when you want to get rid of your lover or break up a couple who shouldn't be together.

What You Need

- Red rose
- Paper with the names of your lover or the couple written on it by you
- 4 nails
- Hammer

Take the paper and dress it with banishing oils or herbs. Garlic, pepper, and sage all work effectively. Fold the paper so it can be enfolded into the petals of the rose. Now find a dead tree and nail your rose/paper combination to it with the four nails. Now beat the flower until it is destroyed. Walk home without casting a backward glance, and your spell is cast.

A White Candle Spell to Attract New Love

This spell is meant for both sexes and is designed to attract love and tenderness. This will not be in the form of a thrall or zombie-like passion, but it will attract all the love that person has for you. This natural form of love is more likely to lead to a successful relationship as it comes from the heart. Accept the level of love you will receive and work on developing your true connections.

What You Need

- An altar or decorated table
- White marriage candle (a plain white 4" altar candle will also work)
- Thorn from a white rose bush

First, decorate your altar or table with objects that symbolize yourself and the object of your love. These can be keepsakes, items of clothing, pictures, and mementos of your time together.

Now take the thorn and inscribe the candle with the phrase *"Come to me, my love"* and the name of the person you want to attract. Repeat until the phrase and the name have been written three times. Burn the candle upon your altar ad visualize your lover coming toward you with loving intentions, completely naked and filled with beauty.

Once the candle has burned down, collect the wax puddle and the other objects from your altar and store them in a safe place. Make sure you know exactly where they are because if you wish to cast off this person in the future, you will need to dispose of the items ceremoniously. Cast the objects and the wax into a fire or bury them at a crossroads to reverse the spell and dispose of any love from this person.

Passion and Lust Spells

Love is great, but sometimes you need to feel baser instincts like lust and passion. These following spells will help you get the oomph back in the bedroom. These spells are great for couples who need some help or can be used to ignite a spark in someone you know but don't have a relationship with.

Casting your spells as the moon is waxing at nine o clock in the evening will make your spell more potent. Performing the spell when the moon is in the house of Taurus will also help your spells' success.

Passion Spell

What You Need

- A clean sterilized pin or needle
- An apple
- Patchouli incense stick

If you perform this spell as a couple, you must both prick your fingers to release a drop of blood. Let the two drops fall on the incense before you light it. If you perform the ritual alone, use two drops of your own blood to symbolize the union.

Light the incense and pass the apple through the smoke three times. Each time you pass, say these words, *"Blood of (your name) mix with the blood of (your partners' name) and become united as one."*

Now slice the apple in half and lay it before the incense stick. The spell is now cast, so prepare yourself for some lustful times ahead!

Easy Lust Spell

This spell is designed to explode euphoric lust between partners that have lost the spark they once had. Use the spell to induce sexual feelings that may have become dormant.

What You Need

- A pink altar candle
- Clean pin
- Rosewater
- Organic honey

This spell will provoke lust in someone to whom you are not romantically attached but who is aware of your presence. Use the pin to etch the name of your potential lover nine times on the candle. Mix the rosewater with a drop of honey and anoint the candle. Don't use too much honey, or the candle will turn into a torch.

Light the candle for nine minutes every night for nine nights.

Once the ritual has finished, wrap the candle's remnants in a piece of red silk and bury it at the foot of a fruit-bearing tree. Your spell is now cast.

These types of spells are some of the most popular magic. Most couples have periods when their relationship is less than perfect, and they need some help. Keeping passion and lust alive when raising a family or working can be difficult. Spells won't fix broken relationships, but they can improve certain areas. Don't try and force people to stay when they know it's time to leave.

Let the negative thoughts you have go before casting your spells. Trust that your magic will work, and the outcome will be the one you hope for. There is always hope and positivity attached to this kind of magic, and you should celebrate this fact. If you have lost confidence in your partnership, then casting a love spell will help you remember why you first loved each other.

Using spells to attract people is a powerful tool, but it needs to be used realistically. Don't try and attract people who are outside of your social circle. Some deluded people try casting spells to attract celebrities and famous people. This won't work. You need to limit your expectations and choose realistic goals.

Chapter 11: Hoodoo Spells for Luck and Wealth

Now we switch the focus from matters of the heart to matters of the pocket. Luck and wealth are always welcome in our lives, and some people believe that luck attracts much more than financial wealth. Lucky people seem to have the best lives. Their friends are great, they have the best jobs and live in the best places. Luck is more than just succeeding in gambling terms. Being lucky means that things just go your way, so why wouldn't we want to attract luck into our lives?

Before you perform these Hoodoo rituals, it is doubly important to create the right space for your work. Luck and wealth will come to you wherever you perform your spells, but if you take the time to set the scene, your spells will be more powerful and bring greater rewards.

Set Up an Altar Designed to Attract Luck and Wealth

This isn't as complicated as it sounds! An altar need not be a complex wooden structure with ornate carvings or a religious tone. Your altar could be as simple as the top of a small cabinet or a table set up in your home. The main thing to remember is an altar should be used only for spells and magic work. You shouldn't use a piece of furniture used daily for other purposes.

Make your altar personal and representative of your beliefs. You can use different colored candles and coverings to indicate your intentions as you perform different types of magic.

When practicing spells to attract luck and wealth, you need to utilize the strength of the color green. Cover your altar with a green cloth and use green colored candles to decorate it.

Charge your space with the four elements by placing a jar of sand to the north, a bowl of water to the west, your green candle to the south, and an incense stick to the east. This represents the power of earth, water, fire, and air.

You can charge your altar with representations of lucky gods and goddesses to improve your work; here are some of the most popular deities:

- Ganesh, the Indian god who represents prosperity and attainment
- Mahakala, the Hindu god of luck and protection
- Bes, an Egyptian god of protection and prosperity
- Jengu are mystical African origin creatures who are incredibly beautiful and bring luck to all who see them
- Felicitas, a Roman goddess of fertility, productivity, and good fortune

This altar charges your tools and surfaces, but more importantly, it charges your spirit with positive energy. The stronger your focus, the more successful your spells will be.

Before you cast any spells regarding wealth or prosperity, focus on improving your luck. Attracting good fortune should be part of your Hoodoo life and should be performed regularly.

A Simple Good Luck Spell

What You Need

- Three green candles
- Incense
- Three acorns

Place the candles into the form of a triangle and place an acorn at each one's base. Light your incense and candles simultaneously.

Recite the following

"Lady Luck and all her handmaidens, I ask for your assistance

Give me the strength of a bear and the luck of a rabbit

I summon the four elements to aid my work

Bring me health and wealth and bring luck to all I do

So be it."

Once the candles have burned down, take the wax and wrap it in green silk before burying it beneath a fruit-bearing tree.

Another simple way to banish bad luck and bring good is to bring a rabbit's foot talisman or amulet to your altar. Place it in the center as you recite this phrase three times *"Bad luck run away from me, you're never welcome here, good luck fortune come to me, you're always welcome here."*

Sprinkle the rabbit's foot with lucky oils like chamomile or lemongrass as you throw a pinch of sacred salt over your left shoulder.

Carry the rabbit's foot with you whenever you feel the need to increase your luck.

How to Attract Wealth and Prosperity Using Hoodoo

The Money Spell

This basic candle spell should be performed over nine days for the most successful results. It can be performed any time of the day but should be repeated at the same time of day for the spell's duration.

What You Need

- A green candle
- A white candle
- Prosperity oil like bergamot, eucalyptus, or jasmine

In this spell, the green candle represents wealth and money, and the white candle represents you. To maximize the power of the spell, you can inscribe the white candle with your name.

Step 1) Charge your candles with the oil you have chosen

Step 2) Place them on your altar nine inches apart

Step 3) Light them both and repeat the following chant

"Money and wealth come to me

In fullness and in plenty three times three

I seek enrichment without harming none

With your help, it will be done

Money, I welcome you three times three."

Step 4) Move the two candles one inch closer to each other

Step 5) Extinguish the candles

Step 6) Repeat the ritual for nine days

Step 7) On the ninth day, let the candles burn to wax before wrapping the remains in a white cloth and placing it in your mojo bag or wallet.

Spell for Business Growth

If you have a business, you know that hard work and long hours are all part of your success. You feel excited and nervous about your business and dedicate all your energy to your business growth dreams. No matter what you do and despite giving 100%, things can still become stuck. This is when you can turn to your Hoodoo learnings to give your business the boost it needs and restore your confidence in the future.

What You Need

- A large plate
- ¼ cup of curd
- Seven coins (include some foreign coins)
- Red mojo bag
- Fast luck oil
- Almond oil
- One green, yellow, red, and blue candle
- A small magnet

First, write the name of your business on a piece of paper and place it under the plate. If you don't have a name yet, write what your intentions and dreams for the business involve.

Carve the symbol of the sun on each candle and anoint them with your oils. Place the curd on top of the plate, then arrange the coins into the shape of a horseshoe. Place the green candle at the top of the plate, the yellow to the right, the blue to the left, and the red at the bottom. Place the magnet in the center of your candles, then light the green candle.

Pray to the gods and goddesses of plenty and ask for their assistance. Now light the yellow candle and repeat your prayers. Follow this with the red and blue candle.

Once the candles have burned down, take the remnants of the curd, the wax, and the coins and place them in your red mojo bag. Carry it with you wherever you go. The spell should be reenergized and repeated every six months or whenever you feel the need.

Remember, there are no freebies in business. All exchanges should be equal, and you need to keep yourself energized. This doesn't mean you can't be generous or helpful but don't overextend yourself or be overly generous.

The Green Candle Money Spell

This simple spell is popular and powerful. Use it to bring wealth and prosperity to your life. Remember, wealth isn't always about finances; it can also mean wealth, knowledge, or love. Good fortune is just as important as financial abundance.

What You Need

- A green candle
- Six coins, two gold, two silver, and two bronze
- A gold cloth
- Jasmine oil

Prepare your altar and take a moment to pray to your favorite deity. Ask for assistance in your magic work, and pray for success. Once you feel charged with energy, begin the spell.

Anoint the candle with your oil and place it in the center of your altar.

Place the six coins around the candle to form a circle of alternate-colored coins,

As you prepare the candle and coins, visualize what you will do with the money or good fortune your spell will attract.

Light your candle while repeating the phrase below three times

"Make the money flow and make my fortunes grow. As the money shines, god fortune will be mine."

Lay out the gold cloth and place the six coins on it. Form a pouch from the cloth while repeating this phrase

"Money comes three by three; all good fortune come to me."

Carry the pouch with you wherever you periodically charge it with your favorite herb or oil to make it work.

The Eight Day Money Bag Spell

Prepare your altar and your positive energies before you start the spell.

What You Need

- A green mojo bag
- Eight coins of different denominations (include foreign coins)
- Eight eucalyptus leaves
- Jasmine oil
- Citrine crystal

Place the coins on your altar and sprinkle them with some of your jasmine oil. Bless them by repeating this phrase eight times:

"Money grows on trees so that riches come to me."

Place the coins, leaves, and crystal in your bag, draw the string tight and bless the bag with the remaining oil.

Everything's Coming Up Aces Spell

What You Need

- An unopened deck of cards
- Breadcrumbs
- Sacred salt

- Silver candle
- Seven coins
- Any lucky metal talisman you love

Open the deck of cards and remove the four aces from the pack. Place them on your altar with the two red aces at north and south and the two black aces at eat and west.

Cover the aces with the breadcrumbs and sacred salt. Scatter the coins around your altar and then place the silver candle in a safe place.

Light the candle and bless your selected talisman before placing it on the altar.

Repeat this phrase three times:

"Aces high or aces low, money and luck to me will flow."

Once the candle has burned down, use the wax to mark the four aces and place them in a safe place.

Dream Job Spell

If you find the cause of your money worries or financial strife is your job, then use this spell to change your career path and earn more money.

What You Need

- Piece of paper and a pen
- Peppermint oil
- Three cloves of garlic
- Silver coin
- Green mojo bag

Write a detailed description of your dream job on the paper. Include salary expectations and a full description of what your duties will be. Sprinkle the peppermint oil on the paper and place it in the bag.

Put the garlic and silver coin in with the bag and repeat the following phrase seven times

> *"Work and love go hand in hand, bless my life with both, help me find the best for me and let my career grow."*

Lucky 7's Ritual for Money and Success

We all know the power of numerology in our Hoodoo workings, and this ritual is a classic example of the strong associations connected to the number 7. Involve your friends and make it into a joint effort to improve everybody's finances.

What You Need

- Eight single dollar bills with 7 as their Federal Reserve number*
- 1 clear quartz crystal
- Iron pyrite stone (also called fool's gold)
- Aventurine quartz

This number is part of the two-digit mark on each dollar note that indicates which bank it originates from. Seven is the number that refers to Chicago, and the 7 will come with a letter. You can choose dollars with a 7 as part of their serial numbers, but the spell won't be as effective.

Take your time to source your dollars and make your spell more potent. Also, the bills should come to you organically over some time. If you go to the bank and ask the teller to source your bills for you, the power of your spell will lessen. Acquiring the bills and showing patience will make you feel more powerful and enthusiastic about the magic you are about to create.

Begin by giving one of your bills to a friend and explaining what you are hoping to achieve. Use your social circle to create a powerful group who are all performing the ritual, and the power of your magic will increase.

Place the remaining seven dollars on your altar or in a silver money clip in a safe place and rest the crystals and stones on top of them. Leave them to charge for seven days.

As your friends begin to gift you with relevant bills, swap them for the bills in your original pile. This fresh injection of energy and magic will help you become even more prosperous and blessed with wealth.

The Full Moon Money Spell

The moon plays a huge part in magical rituals, so it wouldn't be right to omit a spell performed in the moonlight, enhancing its power. Perform this spell under the full moonbeam at midnight, and your spell will become more powerful.

What You Need

- Copper cauldron or similar vessel
- Silver coin
- Peppermint oil
- Sacred salt

Fill the cauldron half full of water. Add the sacred salt and peppermint oil. Place the cauldron directly below the moon's beam and let the lunar power charge the water for thirty minutes before you add the silver coin.

Now recite the following chant three times:

"Powerful lady of the Moon, bring me wealth and make it soon

Share the abundance that you bring and make my life with money ring."

Once the ritual is over, pour the water into the ground and thank it for its help. Place the silver coin in your pocket and keep it with you always.

The main thing to remember when attracting wealth, prosperity, and good luck to your life is to keep your energy levels high and filled with positivity. Use these spells in conjunction with protection powders and herbs to protect your home and yourself from negative forces.

Chapter 12: Daily Hoodoo Routines

No matter what your belief system is, it can be difficult to incorporate your practice into everyday life. Workplaces and other people's homes may not welcome you imposing your beliefs upon others, but that shouldn't mean you need to leave your beliefs at home. There are many ways you can bring your Hoodoo folk magic with you to protect you and bring you luck and love.

When we consider the origins of Hoodoo, it can be easy to forget these folks didn't have a great deal to work with. The slaves that heralded the more powerful aspects of Hoodoo often only had meager kitchen supplies, which they combined with working with the nature surrounding them.

Modern life means you have greater access to manufactured items produced to help perform rituals and spells to improve your lot. However, as with most practices, the old ways are often the most successful, so it is sometimes best to stick to the more traditional blends of herbs and oils to make the magic work.

Ways to Bring Hoodoo Into Your Daily Routine

Most homes have showers in their bathroom, while fewer have bathtubs. Lingering in a bathtub filled with scented water and bubbles is symbolic of luxury rather than everyday washing. So how do you bring the Hoodoo staple ritual of bathing in powders and oils into your life?

We all need to clean ourselves using shower gels or soap, so instead of taking a bath with herbal infusions, you can use soap or gel laced with powerful herbs and oils. The Art of the Root store has some amazing products, including the following.

- The Crown of Success Soap includes High John the Conqueror root, bergamot, vetiver, and other successful herbs and oils
- Come to Me Soap containing jasmine, gardenia, and other love relating herbs and oils for attracting romance and love
- Money drawing soap including cinnamon, chamomile, and other lucky herbs

You can make your own soaps and shower gels to use in your daily routine that your intent and magic will power. Start with an unscented base and add the oils and herbs you favor for a truly magical way to wash.

Having certain Hoodoo waters in your home will also enhance your powers. Florida, Moon, Orange, and Glory waters can be made and kept in your bathroom so you can anoint your body before you set out for the day.

How to Make Hoodoo Waters

The purest forms of blessed waters use rainwater or holy water as a base, while some use alcohol in varying forms. Then add the ingredients you require to make your water magical. Honey, salt, essential oils, and herbs can all be added to make your version of Hoodoo water.

Keep the waters in spray bottles clearly labeled with the type of power it holds. Spray it as you would room for freshening sprays. Anoint doors and windows to keep your house a powerfully safe place and attract good luck and prosperity.

A Typical Recipe for Florida Water

One of the most multi-functional waters available is Florida Hoodoo water

What You Need

- 17 ounces Vodka, cheap stuff works just and expensive, so don't waste the good vodka in your drink's cabinet
- Fresh mint
- Fresh basil
- Dried jasmine
- Dried lavender
- Lemon peel
- One cinnamon stick
- A clove
- Allspice berries

Place the vodka in a copper saucepan and heat it for 10 minutes on low heat. Add the ingredients and simmer for 40 minutes. Bottle when cooled and enjoy!

Florida water can be used as a cologne or perfume that smells great and is a powerful connection to your Hoodoo beliefs.

Your Mojo Bag and Why You Should Always Carry One With You

Your mojo bag is a highly personal piece of magic, so why would you leave it out of your daily routine? Although you need to keep it secret, there is always a way to carry it with you. Always keep a small version on your person and charge it with your favorite herbs and keepsakes.

Make bags for all occasions and keep them in your personal space. If you need protection or help with romance, choose the bag that will help you the most. Think of your mojo bag as an invisible force keeping you safe and improving your life.

State Your Intentions

Hoodoo doesn't rely on objects and rituals to work. These aspects of rootwork will enhance your magic, but your intentions are the most important part of your work. These fuel your soul and power your life, so it's important to get them out there into the world so they can be heard.

Never be afraid to state your intentions clearly and with a steady tone. If you feel your work is undervalued, then tell someone. Does your partner neglect the housework and rely on you too much? Tell them. You shouldn't have to rely on magic and spells to make your intentions come to fruition.

You can give them a helping hand with Hoodoo. Write down your intentions before you attend important meetings and use the paper to gain the upper hand. If you want a promotion, write down what your new title will be nine times on a piece of paper and wear it on your person when attending the interview.

Amulets and talismans are also a powerful way to carry your intentions with you. Carve a more permanent reminder of what you want on a stone or a piece of bark and carry it in your pocket. Paper intentions are okay for short-term intentions, but a stone or other natural materials work better in the long run.

Timing

We have already discovered how the moon and its position in the sky affect Hoodoo's work, but there are other considerations to ponder. The time of day is a key factor when performing your work and magic. If you perform a spell to repel things or diminish threats, perform your work as the minute hand is traveling down (e.g., from 12 o'clock to 12.30.) If your spell is to attract, then perform it as the minute hand travels upward (e.g., from 11:30 to 12 o'clock.)

Time is an auspicious part of Hoodoo, and when you bring that knowledge into your everyday life, you can draw energy from all aspects. The prime hours for Hoodoo work are 2, 9, 11, and 12 o clock, both in the am and pm, and the hours between 4 and 7 o clock. Schedule your day around these hours, and you will benefit from an increased sense of positivity and power.

Food and Drink Related to Hoodoo

When you think about your day and how to bring your beliefs to your home or life, then mealtimes must be considered. We all eat, and food helps us connect to other people and form bonds. Sitting at a family dining table sharing dishes with loved ones is a special experience. Sharing food with friends can make an ordinary get-together into a memorable time.

Bringing the essence of Hoodoo and folk magic to the table will help you connect to the ancestors and improve your links to those who practiced the craft before you. This can be as simple a process as adding some of those tasty herbs you use in magic to make your food taste better, or it can be full dishes that originate from slave roots and the concept of soul food.

Here are Some Herbs That are Guaranteed to Improve Your Food

- For love add bay leaves, cardamom, dill, and frangipani
- For protection, add anise, fennel, juniper, and rosemary
- For luck, add allspice, cinnamon, nutmeg, and orange

If you love to experiment in the kitchen, why not try some recipes that originate from the early Hoodoo communities. You will improve your taste buds and feed your soul.

If you fancy eating outside but are bored with the traditional BBQ dishes you regularly serve, try this seafood boil. All the family can get involved, and the history behind the dish will fascinate them. Back in the day, lots of people ate catfish and combined the fish with other commonly found seafood to create a huge pot of tasty food to feed their families and friends.

Seafood Boil

Ingredients

- 160 cups of water
- 2 sliced lemons
- 2 sweet onions
- 3 sprigs of parsley, thyme, and dill
- 8 small cloves of garlic
- ½ cup of salted butter
- 1 tbsp cider
- 2 tbsp garlic powder
- 2 tbsp salt
- 1 tbsp onion powder
- 1 tbsp dried oregano
- 3 lb. crab legs
- 2 lb. of prepared shrimp

- 1 lb. crabs' claws
- 4 lobster tails
- 2 lb. smoked sausage
- 8 corn cobs sliced into three parts
- 6 potatoes

Directions

1) Take a large pot capable of holding all your ingredients and place it on the stove

2) Check all the seafood and herbs are clean and free from shells and stalks

3) Chop both of your onions and both lemons and throw them in the pot

4) Add the water, herbs, garlic, butter, cider, and the dried ingredients to the pot

5) Boil the water and then reduce the heat to a medium setting

6) Cook for 45 minutes and then remove all the detritus from your herbs

7) Add the sausage, corn, and potato and cook for 15 minutes

8) Add all the seafood except the shrimp and cook for 10 minutes

9) Add the shrimp and turn the heat off

10) Let it sit for 10 minutes before serving

Take the pot out to the garden and serve it to your guests. Have plenty of newspaper or paper towels ready for cleaning your fingers, and then dig in! Let the kids and adults fish out the tasty claws and lobster tails and dip them in a garlic sauce or a zesty lemon sauce and accompany the dish with some traditional cornbread.

Cornbread Recipe

Ingredients

- 1 cup cornmeal
- 1 cup all-purpose flour
- 1/3 cup of sugar
- 1 tbsp baking powder
- ½ tsp salt
- 2 eggs
- ¼ cup of melted salted butter
- 1 cup full-fat milk

1) Preheat the oven to 400 degrees F

2) Prepare a greased dish or pan

3) Beat milk, eggs, and butter in a large bowl

4) Add remaining ingredients and mix until the batter is smooth

5) Cook for 20-25 minutes until the bread is a golden-brown color

You can add other ingredients to your bread to make it tasty. Jalapeno peppers and chili flakes are great if you prefer a kick with your cornmeal bread.

Hoecake

Legend tells us that enslaved people cooked these corn cakes on their hoes in the field as a mid-day snack. Some slaves had use of a griddle in the hearth called a hoe, while others baked them on a board facing their fires.

Ingredients

- 1 cup stone-ground cornmeal
- ¾ cup of boiling water

- ½ tsp salt
- ¼ cup of shortening, lard, vegetable oil, or beef tallow

1) Mix the salt and corn flour in a bowl

2) Melt the shortening in a skillet or frying pan

3) Take a tbsp of batter and add it to the hot fat

4) Fry until firm and light brown

5) Drain on paper towels before serving them warm with butter or honey

Sweet potatoes, okra, chitlins, and pigs' feet were stapled parts of Hoodoo fare, and they can be used to enhance your dining table today. Food is the perfect way to marry your beliefs with your everyday life.

Sweet Potato Casserole

This everyday filling dish is perfect for including all your favorite ingredients and herbs.

Ingredients

- 4 large, sweet potatoes
- 2 beaten eggs
- 4 tbsp butter
- ½ cup milk
- ½ tsp vanilla extract
- ½ cup all-purpose flour
- ½ cup crushed nuts to garnish
- ½ cup butter
- ½ cup sugar

1) Preheat the oven to 325 F while cooking the sweet potatoes in salted water for 15 minutes or until soft

2) Add the cooked potatoes to the milk, butter, and vanilla extract. Season to taste and add required herbs

3) Mix until smooth

4) Make the topping by combining the flour, sugar, and butter and add the nuts

5) Place the potato mix in a baking dish and top with the topping

6) Bake for 30 minutes until the top is crispy

What Better Than a Sweet Tea to Accompany Your Hoodoo-Based Food?

Here are some traditional sweet teas that are both tasty and healthy. The sweetness comes from the actual tea as opposed to sugar. The sweetness originates from the leaves and compounds in the roots of the plant and is a perfect way to bring Hoodoo roots to the table.

Rooibos

Also known as African red bush tea, this is one of the most versatile herbal drinks in the world. Drink it hot or cold and use it to make your favorite latte tastier and healthier. The sweet taste and lack of caffeine make it a perfect drink to serve children.

Licorice Root

This root-based tea is strictly for people with a real sweet tooth. Imagine candy melted in hot water that can be drunk guilt-free. That is what licorice root tea tastes like. Enjoy it as it comes, or add some of your favorite Hoodoo herbs to make the taste more personal.

Chamomile

One of the most available forms of herbal teas, not all brands taste the same. The best types of chamomile tea have a deep yellow hue with a subtle sweet taste.

Cinnamon

This tea is for people who prefer a spicier drink but don't mind a touch of sweetness. Source teas made from the bark of the plant for a more intense flavor.

Black Tea

If you want a sweet version of this mainly Indian type of tea, choose Chinese brands like Golden Monkey. The plants used for this tea have yellow buds that bring a hint of chocolate and honey to the brew.

Conclusion

So, now you know the power and magic contained in the learnings of Hoodoo. You can now attract love and wealth while protecting yourself against your enemies. Use your new powers carefully and always respect the guidelines that accompany the folk magic you use.

There are opportunities to misuse magic, and you can cause distress and pain to others, but you should be guided by your conscience and social conventions. You can bring happiness and love to your world and others, so concentrate on the good you can bring. Good luck with your magic, and remember to pay respects to the ancestors who formed the craft.

Part 2: Voodoo

Unlocking the Hidden Power of Haitian Vodou and New Orleans Voodoo

Introduction

What comes into your mind when you hear about Voodoo and its spells? Are you one of those who believe that it is a depiction of dark witchcraft or black magic that can harm someone? Then it is time to those misconceptions! Note that while it has garnered a bad reputation due to its portrayal in pop culture, it is not as evil as most people have claimed it to be.

To know more about Voodoo, you should open yourself up to the truth; it is inaccurate to describe it as just *dark magic*. It is not all about working with the devil and evil spirits to trigger harm to someone. Contrary to how the movies and TV shows present it, you can't tie it to evil's diabolical acts, puppets, and zombies.

Voodoo is more than those evil misrepresentations and misconceptions; it is a religion with deep roots. Voodoo practitioners place this religion in high regard. The practice is important to them, and they do not look at it as an instrument for torture, cannibalism, and devil worship.

To finally unlock the real power of Voodoo, rather than the historical misunderstandings and misrepresentations surrounding it, then this book will serve as your ultimate source of information. It is up-to-date and aims to correct all the misinformation and misconceptions about this specific religion that many practitioners love.

The good thing about this book is that it contains information that is easy to absorb and understand. Even beginners and those who are unfamiliar with Voodoo can quickly grasp the concepts. To learn more about Voodoo spells, you can also refer to this book as its steps and instructions are simple and easy to apply. By the time you have reached the end of this book, you will understand Voodoo's secrets and correct the misconceptions others strongly believe in. Now, let's begin your journey toward learning more about Voodoo and unraveling its secrets!

Chapter 1: The Voodoo Twins - Haiti and New Orleans

Voodoo refers to a monotheistic and syncretic religion, which resulted from the combined religions of the native Africans and Roman Catholics. Mainly practiced in New Orleans and Haiti, you can see Voodoo being recognized in other locations, too, particularly in the Caribbean.

Voodoo has several definitions. The most socially acceptable and common one is that it is the act of worshipping more than just one God. It also worships spirits, ancestors, saints, and angels. This practice combines Catholic saint worship, witchcraft, Native American practices, and folk magic.

Contrary to what most people believe, Voodoo does not solely revolve around dark witchcraft and black magic to harm people. Most of the real practitioners of Voodoo state you can't do evil spirit worship here. So, it is time to finally set the record straight and understand that this practice is not as evil as others have claimed and believed it to be.

The spells associated with Voodoo are useful, powerful, and authentic. You can expect them to work effectively in various circumstances – among them are in the fields of finances, career, relationships, and love. However, it is safe to say that this religion has extensive coverage. Provided you use and practice it correctly, you can improve various aspects of yourself and your life through it.

How Voodoo Started

The original roots of Voodoo can be traced back to Africa. It was brought to America by the African slaves after they were sold to white slave traders. Specifically, Voodoo started after the slaves in Africa carried their native traditions upon their forceful transport to the New World.

During that time, they were prohibited from practicing their faith and religion. With the restrictions and prohibitions set in place, these African slaves began equating the Gods they knew with the saints recognized in the Roman Catholic Church. They did that to sidestep the restrictions associated with the practice of their religions.

It also prompted them to do rituals with the help of the imagery and items used by and recognized in the Catholic Church. They incorporated the beliefs of the Catholics into their religious practices. Most believed it was the only way for them to continue practicing what they initially believed in. After all, restrictions meant they had to hide their former religious practices. They also did that because Voodoo naturally allowed them to incorporate saints into their practice.

When African slaves were moved to the New World, it was one of the darkest periods in world history. It was also when Voodoo contributed to helping everyone feel what it was like to be free – even if they did not have the right to practice freedom yet.

African Voodoo

Of course, you would not completely understand Voodoo if you do not dig deeper into its roots. As mentioned earlier, this practice started in Africa. It began in Fon and Kongo, known as African kingdoms, around six thousand years back. The term, *Voodoo*, was even derived from the Fon language. It means *deity, spirit, or sacred*.

Presently, Fon is part of Southern Benin, a region referred to by many anthropologists as Voodoo's cradle. Millions of people continue practicing Voodoo even today, especially in Ghana, Togo, and other Northwestern African countries.

Voodoo is mainly an oral tradition. With that in mind, you will notice several differences and changes in the names of gods and the specific ways rituals are performed in various regions and generations. African Voodoo, however, demonstrates a few consistent qualities regardless of where it is practiced.

Aside from believing in spiritual possession and several gods, African Voodoo also differs. It consistently venerates or worships ancestors, using particular objects or rituals to spread magical protection. It also offers animal sacrifices to show respect to a god, ask for favors, or show their gratitude.

Africans also practice Voodoo by using fetishes and certain items with the power or essence of specific spirits. Ceremonial instruments, music, and dances that use elaborate masks and costumes are common in African Voodoo practice. Moreover, they do divination by interpreting physical activities.

You can also see most of its practitioners associating foods, colors, plants, and other objects, with a certain Loa, a Voodoo spirit designed to offer guidance in various aspects of life, like spirituality, healing, protection, success, sexuality, and death.

Most qualities and traits mentioned, especially those related to polytheism, ancestor worship, and dance and music, are also vital aspects of other religions practiced in Africa. With that in mind, you can look at Voodoo as similar to other traditional religions in the country.

Most observances also look like they are partly religious service and celebration with rhythmic music, songs, and dances. Several rituals performed in African Voodoo also use natural landscapes, including trees, mountains, and rivers.

African Voodoo turns the most mundane objects, such as bottles, pots, or slaughtered animals' body parts, into something sacred they can use in rituals. This is possible through the consecration and decoration of the said objects.

Introduction to Voodoo's Most Important Branches

Now that you know how Africans practice Voodoo, it is time to know more about the two most important branches - the Haiti Vodou and the New Orleans Voodoo. The two branches were derived from a religious belief brought to America by the African slaves, so you can expect them to be similar.

It is still crucial to understand each branch separately, so you have a clear idea of what makes the two similar and different and how both originated.

The Haitian Vodou

Haitian Vodou started around the 16th and 19th centuries. It was developed in Afro-Haitian communities when the Atlantic slave trade occurred during those times. It began after combining traditional religions carried by the slaves in West Africa to the Hispaniola Island with the teachings spread by French colonialists regarding the Roman Catholic religion. The French colonialists had full control of the island.

Many of those who practiced Vodou participated in the Haitian Revolution that occurred between 1791 and 1804. It was when they contributed to conquering the government ruled by the French colonialists. It also contributed to abolishing slavery and the founding of what we can view as modern-day Haiti.

When they were still slaves, a code prevented them from practicing the religion they usually practiced. The slave code even required them to convert into Christians. This prompted them to get forcefully baptized as Christians, hugely influencing how they practiced Vodou.

The fact that the slaves were prohibited from observing and practicing their religion freely and openly caused them to borrow several elements of the Roman Catholics as a means of protecting their spiritual beliefs and practices. It resulted in the execution of the syncretization process, which had a major impact on the practice of Voodoo in Haiti.

After the Haitian Revolution, the church governed by the Roman Catholics also left the island. For a few decades, the absence of Catholics resulted in Vodou turning into Haiti's most dominant religion. During the 20th century, the increasing emigration rate caused Vodou to spread to other parts of the world.

In the latter part of the 20th century, people noticed a significantly growing connection between Vodou and some relevant traditions in the Americas, like Brazilian Candomblé and Cuban Santeria, and traditions practiced in West Africa.

Common Beliefs in Haitian Vodou

One thing noticeable about Haitian Vodou is that it has no central institutional authority and liturgy. It also has communal and domestic variations. You will notice several variations in this community, particularly in its manner of practice in urban and rural areas and how it is executed in Haiti and in the global Haitian diaspora.

You will also notice variations in beliefs and practices from one congregation to another. One variation would be an extended family being a significant component of a single congregation. Other common beliefs of Haitian Vodou include:

Bondyé and Loa (Lwa)

Haitian Vodou is mainly a monotheistic religion as it teaches the presence and existence of only one supreme God. This supreme entity built the universe, which Vodou practitioners recognize as Bondyé. Most practitioners also call Bondyé being transcendent and remote, a God who does not want to get involved in the everyday affairs of humans.

With that in mind, they also believe there is no point in directly approaching Bondyé. Instead, what Haitians often do is state "si Bondyé vie," which means "if Bondyé is willing" in their rituals. This is to signify their firm belief that everything will take place based on the will of the deity rather than on their needs expressed through prayer.

Vodou is also recognized as a polytheistic religion, teaching practitioners that a Loa (Lwa), a pantheon of deities, exists. This term refers to spirits, geniuses, or Gods that most Haitian Vodou practitioners believe in. There are also instances when Lwa's are viewed as the counterparts of angels in Christian cosmology. With that, they can offer protection, advice or counsel, and help to humans, provided they participate in ritual services.

All Vodou practitioners also regard Lwa as Bondyé's intermediaries – with each one of them displaying a unique personality. They also associate or link each Lwa to a specific color, object, and day of the week.

Other Famous Beliefs

Haitian Vodou also believes in ethics and morality and that every gender has unique and different roles to play. Being a recognized religion, it mirrors the daily concerns of people. It also focuses on providing techniques that will help mitigate misfortunes and illnesses. Practitioners also believe those who do everything to survive are among the most highly ethical people.

In terms of morality, you will notice that Haitian Vodou does not implement too many rules. This means that the morality in this religion is not solely based on rules, but rather it is contextual based on the situation and the person subjected to it. According to Haitian Vodou followers, they consider someone as morally upright if he lives in accordance with his real character and the tutelary Loa (Lwa).

Aside from that, they put a lot of emphasis on conformity, support, group cohesion, and uniformity. The religion tries to strengthen family ties. They also emphasize showing respect to the elderly and view the extended family as a highly vital part of Haitian society. Most followers and practitioners of the religion do not also tolerate Maji, the term used to describe the process of using supernatural powers for evil and self-serving purposes.

Common Practices

Haitian Vodou can be viewed as a religion composed of influences derived from several other religions. Despite the numerous obvious additions and integrations, Haitian Voodoo still strongly resembles the Voodoo practiced initially in Africa. For instance, they have designations for those who will carry out religious services and activities and offer traditional folk remedies, namely the houngans (priests) and mambos (priestesses).

Anyone who intends to serve as a houngan (or mambo) needs to participate in an apprenticeship program. They have to act as initiates with other recognized leaders in the community instead of just participating in a worship center. There is also what is referred to as *honfour* in Voodoo, which is where ceremonies occur. It is, therefore, the counterpart of a sanctuary or temple in other religions.

Aside from that, there are also other aspects of Haitian Voodoo that make their practice more recognizable. These include:

• **Spiritual Possession** - Similar to the Voodoo practiced in Africa, Haitian Voodoo also considers possession one of its most vital aspects. Practitioners refer to a person possessed as a horse with the possessing Lwa riding on it. One thing that helps them identify the possessed is when he/she has unnatural movements, speaks using unknown/unfamiliar languages, or delivers direct and clear statements to others who practice and follow the religion.

• **Sacrifice and Offerings** - Another element you will most commonly see in Haitian Voodoo is sacrifice. You can see them sacrificing animals, like chickens and goats, in various ceremonies. The reason is that Vodou strongly believes how important it is to feed the Loa (Lwa). Food offerings and drinks are just some rituals commonly practiced in the religion. They often do it at home or in communal spaces.

There is also a yearly feast (organized by a mambo or oungan) for the congregation, requiring congregants to sacrifice certain animals and offer them to the Lwa. Those who practice the religion also offer drinks and foods based on the exact Lwa they want to dedicate the feast or ritual to. Note that every Loa

(Lwa) has different food preferences, so it is crucial to offer those they prefer during the ritual.

For instance, Danbala prefers white foods, notably eggs. There is also a Lwa known as Legba who wants any food served to him, whether vegetables, tubers, or meat, to be grilled.

• **Ritual Objects and Clothing** – Haitian Voodoo also makes a point to include certain objects, decorations, and clothing in their rituals and celebrations. Most of these items are also used to show how they respect the Lwa. Several also use Kongo (medicine) packets to hold items and herbs with medicinal or healing properties.

Many worshippers bring drapo (flags) with them all the time to demonstrate their respect for the spirits. You will also notice many using and playing various drums, rattles, and bells to invoke and calling the Lwa.

Other ritual items and objects used by those who practice Haitian Voodoo are decorated bottles, calabashes usually filled with food offerings, and dolls. They often put these items on altars. A few of these objects are now major components of Haitian crafts and artworks.

• **Altars and Shrines** – Haitian Vodou followers also practice their faith and belief with altars and shrines. Several altars even hold lithographs of saints recognized in the Roman Catholic religion. During the time chromolithography was developed, it immediately influenced the imagery used in Vodou. It resulted in the widespread access of images of saints derived from the Roman Catholic Church with their corresponding Loa (Lwa).

Vodou practitioners also made it a point to use various materials available to them to make shrines. There are also certain places, aside from the temples, that practitioners used when performing rituals. For instance, they often perform rituals in cemeteries, making the perfect place for rituals, particularly for those who want to approach and talk to dead spirits.

Many practitioners also choose crossroads as the perfect spot for rituals. The reason is that these are points that provide access to the world of the spirits. It is also possible to use Christian churches, markets, fields, the sea, and rivers for a Vodou ritual.

- **Healing** - Healing is also a common and essential practice in Vodou. The practitioners usually receive amulets and charms from oungan and Mambo. Also known as pwen or points, these charms and amulets are often based on plants known for their healing powers.

Usually a bath, which uses various ingredients that aid in healing, will be prescribed. Haiti also has several herb doctors offering herbal remedies to treat a wide range of ailments. However, these herb doctors are different as mambo and oungan, so expect certain limitations regarding the issues they can heal or handle.

- **Pilgrimage and Festivals** - Haitian Vodou also practice celebrating birthdays for a specific Loa (Lwa). This regularly happens when the Roman Catholics hold the All Souls and All Saints days. These celebrations require them to dedicate special altars designed for the Lwa whose birthday they want to celebrate.

They also honor the dead by holding celebrations that are often conducted in Port au Prince's cemeteries. This celebration comes in a festival with participants dressing up in a way associated with death. Some outfits, therefore, are purple and black coats, sunglasses, top hats, and black veils.

You can also see pilgrimage being a significant part of the culture of Haitian Vodou. Those who undertake the Haitian pilgrimage usually need to wear colored ropes around the waist or head.

Voodoo has now become an integral part of several Haitians' daily lives and activities, as over half of the Haitian population practices this religion. It is also the reason it has a crucial role in the history of the place.

The Louisiana (New Orleans Voodoo)

The second most important branch of Voodoo we have to talk about is the Louisiana Voodoo, otherwise called the *New Orleans Voodoo*. This specific branch refers to a collection of spiritual practices and beliefs all developed based on the traditions followed by the African diaspora within Louisiana.

This Voodoo can also be defined as the cultural variation of the Afro-American religion developed within the Creole, Spanish, and French-speaking Afro-American population in the state. Louisiana Voodoo is one out of the numerous African-based religion incarnations that came from West African Dahomeyan Vodun. It was synchronized with the Roman Catholic religion and the Francophone culture famous in South Louisiana due to the trade of slaves.

While many confuse Louisiana Voodoo with Haitian Vodou, they are different. The one from Louisiana emphasizes using Gris-gris, Hoodoo occult paraphernalia, snake deity or the Li Grand Zombi, and voodoo queens. Louisiana Voodoo even played a role in introducing gris-gris and voodoo dolls in America's culture.

How did it Start?

New Orleans or Louisiana voodoo came because of the enslaved West Africans who made it a point to merge their religious practices and rituals with the local Roman Catholic population. One important fact about New Orleans or Louisiana voodoo is that it strongly connects with the spirits, ancestors, and nature.

Voodoo was bolstered even more after its followers, who escaped from Haitian Revolution in 1791, moved to New Orleans. During this time, those who practiced Voodoo in North American colonies lived more complicated lives. The French colonists implemented more aggressive measures to suppress their rituals and avoid future uprisings. This is mainly because it was said that the revolution started after a Vodou ritual triggered slaves to be possessed by a deity.

Unlike their time in Haiti, the slaves who moved to Louisiana were not aggressive or rebellious against their masters. What they did, instead, was use charms and amulets to make their everyday lives easier. These Voodoo practitioners and followers used these items primarily for protection, healing, and guidance. They also believed that the charms and amulets were among the things that connected them with the people they loved. There were also charms believed to hurt their enemies. These items are what they used when making curses.

The slaves continuing to practice Voodoo turned into an extremely important part of the New Orleans culture. You can even see voodoo kings and queens becoming political and spiritual figures of the 1800s New Orleans power. It also caused the spread of the religion in other places, like across the Mississippi Valley, that still reported famous voodoo ceremonies up to 1891.

New Orleans (Louisiana Voodoo) Major Beliefs

One major belief linked to the New Orleans (Louisiana) Voodoo is there is only one God who will never interfere or intercede with people's lives. Most of them believe that the spirits can preside and interfere with one's life. New Orleans or Louisiana voodoo practitioners believe that the spiritual forces are either mischievous or kind and capable of shaping their daily lives by interceding and interfering with them.

With that, they strongly recognize the importance of connecting with spirits. They can do that through music, dance, and singing. It is also possible to establish a spiritual connection by using snakes that mainly represent Legba, the spiritual conduit to all the others. The Voodoo serpent symbolizes not only healing knowledge but also the strong connection between the Earth and Heaven.

Singing is also a vital part of performing voodoo rituals. Practitioners sing to show how they worship God and the spirits. Usually, you can witness them singing while also clapping, stomping their feet, and patting. Drum playing was also part of the ritual when they were still slaves, and they did that only during the public ceremony held in Congo Square every week.

The songs played in rituals often describe the unique personalities of each deity. They mention the deity names, their origins, likes and dislikes, strengths, weaknesses, and responsibilities. Several songs reflect the tunes used in the Roman Catholic Church, and there is a connection between the saints in that religion with the deities famous in Africa.

Aside from songs (music) and dance, New Orleans Voodoo also uses gris-gris dolls, talismans, and potions. You can still find these items in households and stores throughout the city. This reminds everyone of the fascination of New Orleans, with not only spirits but also mystery and magic.

They also practice Voodoo through spiritual baths, personal ceremonies, prayer, and readings. Nowadays, those who continue to practice it also believe that it is a significant help in curing anxiety, depression, loneliness, and addictions. Many also use it to offer help to the sick, hungry, and poor.

Famous Characters in New Orleans Voodoo

New Orleans Voodoo also introduced a few of the most famous characters to the world. There are famous Voodoo queens who make up the religion's most influential female practitioners, and they are known for exercising their immense power in communities. These led the majority of ritual dances and ceremonial meetings.

Among the most powerful and famous names in New Orleans Voodoo are the following:

Marie Laveau

Marie Laveau (1794 to 1881) was the most popular Voodoo queen during her time. Many even call her the most powerful and eminent of the many voodoo queens in New Orleans. Even the wealthiest people, planters, businessmen, lawyers, and politicians approached her to ask her advice. They asked for her opinions whenever they needed to decide on business-related and financial matters. Laveau also made it a point to help the enslaved and the poor.

Laveau was so powerful that she dominated even the other renowned leaders of Voodoo in New Orleans. She was also a devout Catholic, so she urged her people to participate in the Catholic mass celebration. With her strong influence, it was no longer surprising to witness Roman Catholic practices being adopted into Voodoo's belief system.

People also remember her for how she showed compassion for the poor and less fortunate. Besides that, it was discovered that she was fond of filling her home with images of the saints, candles, items, and altars designed to keep it protected from spirits.

Even up to the present, Voodoo practitioners recognize Laveau's role in the practice of their religion. As a matter of fact, her gravesite became a tourist attraction. Voodoo practitioners and believers even continue to send gifts to her gravesite. She continues to be a prominent figure in Louisiana Voodoo and a major part of the entire culture of New Orleans.

Doctor John

If there is a famous queen in Voodoo, there is also Dr. John, who is the most popular king in New Orleans Voodoo. Born in Senegal, Dr. John was kidnapped and brought to Cuba as a slave. Later on, he moved to New Orleans, where he participated in the Voodoo community.

It was during this time when his skills in Voodoo's medicinal aspects were recognized. People saw him as an incredible healer. Many believed that he could resurrect even those dying patients through Voodoo rituals. He eventually became Marie Laveau's teacher and is recognized today as one of the most prominent leaders in Louisiana Voodoo.

The Modern New Orleans Voodoo

At present, many still practice Voodoo in New Orleans. Practitioners do it mainly to offer their service to others. Many also perform Voodoo to influence life events as they connect to spirits and ancestors.

Usually, Voodoo practitioners hold rituals privately. You can also find a lot of places that provide ritual assistance and readings. New Orleans even has a formally established temple for Voodoo, the Voodoo Spiritual Temple, that you can find across Congo Square.

You can also find museums in the city where you can learn about New Orleans Voodoo history and their famous rituals, altars, and artifacts. Voodoo in the city was even commercialized during the early parts of the 21st century.

Commercial interests pursued the capitalization of the strong interest of people in this religion. You can even see shops selling gris-gris, powders, candles, and charms today that cater to the needs of practitioners and tourists who want to learn more about Voodoo.

Chapter 2: Bondye and the Voodoo Gods

Like many other pagan spiritual and belief systems, Voodoo practitioners also believe in different deities, spirits, Gods, and various Divine aspects. The belief is often based on the worldview of the practitioners and worshippers. With its different regional strains, like Haitian, New Orleans, Hoodoo, and Mississippi Valley, you may find this practice confusing. Still, you can make it a lot easier to understand by looking closely at each system's fundamental principles.

One way to do that is to learn about the deities that the systems and strains have in common and the similar energies they share. An important fact about Voodoo that can help you understand it even better, despite its numerous variations, is that it is a monotheistic religion.

This means that its followers believe in just one god. It is where Bondye comes into the picture as He is the Supreme Being that the Voodoo practitioners firmly have faith in. While they interact and communicate more with Lwa (Loa) or the spirits, it is the good God, Bondye, that they consider holding the highest power in their spiritual realm.

For practitioners to practice Voodoo without worrying about acceptance by society, the deities and Lwa (spirits) related to the Christian and Catholic hierarchy have to be recognized. By doing that, it would appear that they are petitioning a specific saint known in the Catholic religion when they are, in fact, communicating with a Voodoo Pantheon member. This is understandable when you look into the history of slavery and the subterfuge used for slaves to continue their religious practices.

Some connections to the Roman Catholic saints are clear and obvious. One example is St. Patrick, known to be the saint who cast out the snakes of Ireland. This saint was linked to Dambulla, which is known as Lwa in Voodoo.

St. Peter and the Lwa Papa Legba are also connected, considering that the two were the trusted ones to hold keys. Similar to St. Peter, with the keys to both heaven and Hell, Papa Legba is the one you have to invoke to reach other Lwas.

Bondye Is the Supreme Being

In the Voodoo religion, only one God is considered supreme, and that is Bondye. He is called the creator God you can easily recognize as part of the Voodoo religion. He is also the Pantheon's head. As the only supreme God, the Lwa (Loa) or spirits are answerable to Him. These spirits even need to act as intermediaries between this supreme God and humans.

With Bondye holding superior power among all the deities and spirits known in Voodoo, His existence is so profound that humans can't comprehend it. His name, Bondye, was derived from the French term "Bon Deu, which means "The Good God." He got such a title even if he has no evil counterpart in the realm of Vodou deities.

In Voodoo, you can measure a person's "good" based on how much their actions increase or reduce the power of Bondye. This means that prosperity, happiness, and freedom that make a community stronger while protecting life are good for mankind. Those that tend to destroy these things are considered bad.

Similar to the Abrahamic God in Jewish, Islamic, and Christian religions, Bondye is also remote. He is inaccessible, which is why your requests for help, development, and assistance, and your prayers, should not only be aimed at the other deities but also other aspects closely linked to the Earth plane.

It would be like directing your rituals and prayers, including the lighting of candles, to the involved saints with certain areas of influence. Following what the Voodoo practitioners believe in, Bondye is also known as the universe's superior principle.

Recognized as the creator God, He holds responsibility for maintaining human activity and universal order. This God is also recognized as the wholeness of the whole of humanity. It is from Him that all forms of life come. All human lives also belong to him.

Voodoo and the Lwas

Loa or Lwas refer to the spirits recognized in both Louisiana and Haitian Voodoo. They are the ones that all Voodoo believers communicate and interact with. Also spelled as Loa, it encompasses the main spirits who form part of any Voodoo variation. The term was derived from *loi,* a French word, which means *law.* It got such a name because each spirit represents a law of the human condition or law of nature.

You can liken these spirits to the Yoruba religion's orishas and the similar new religious movements of the Afro-Caribbean. Lwa can also be differentiated from orishas because the former can't be categorized as deities but spirits, whether they originated from the divine or humans. Bondye created these spirits so that the living would receive help and assistance in their daily affairs.

Lwas serves as the intermediaries between Bondye and humanity, considering this supreme creator is recognized for being distant from the world and humanity. One thing to note about Lwas is that they are not like angels and saints you simply have to pray to; you must serve them.

Lwas are forces of nature, but you can also expect them to have their own personal mythologies and unique personalities. Each is distinct, so they have their individual likes and dislikes, particular modes of service, and unique sacred songs, rhythms, ritual symbols, and dances.

It is also through a particular Lwa that Bondye can manifest his will. They are spirits capable of manifesting as forces with a huge impact on people's everyday lives. Remembering that, you will notice Voodoo ceremonies mainly focus on Lwa instead of Bondye. Those who practice this religion offer something to the Lwas. Aside from that, these spirits usually possess practitioners, making it possible for them to interact and communicate directly with the community.

Sometimes, those who are unfamiliar with Voodoo refer to Lwas as Gods. This is a mistake, though. Remember that they are mainly spirits who serve as intermediaries between Bondye and the physical world.

Venerating or Worshipping the Lwa

For most Voodoo practitioners and devotees, the Lwa has a major influence on their lives. They firmly believe that they have an intense and demanding but fulfilling relationship with the Lwa. As devotees, they offer their service to these spirits who they respect not only and love but also fear. They regard the Lwa with high respect.

One method of showing respect is adding the prefix Papa, which means father, Maman, which means mother, and Maitresse, which means mistress, whenever they refer to a Lwa. By showing their piety and devotion to the Lwa they believe in, they also expect to receive protection, favors, and blessings from them in return.

Voodoo practitioners also show their devotions and respect to the Lwas by holding ceremonies. During these ceremonies, they can show clearly how intense their relationship is to the Lwas they have faith in. These ceremonies equal religious services they often perform inside an ounfò with the Vodou houngan (priest) or mambo (priestess) facilitating them.

The place where the ceremony is held also comes with a peristyle, which is a semi-open space often situated at the entrance. The central part of it is where the practitioners perform their public rituals. You will also notice a pillar in the middle that features a beautifully designed spiraling snake. With this pillar, the ground gets connected to the ceiling.

It is in this pillar where the Lwa will either descend or ascend. With that, it is safe to say that this pillar, otherwise called *potomitan*, has a crucial role whenever Voodoo ceremonies occur. This pillar also has a strong connection with Papa Legba (the crossroads' keeper) and Danbala.

Each Voodoo ceremony, which aims to call upon a Lwa, involves a lot of dancing, songs, and music, spiritual drawings or vèvè tracing, and drumming, and prayers. These activities are meant to invite the Lwa to participate in the ceremony, join the living, and receive and accept any sacrifice or offering that the devotees present.

One sign of successfully calling upon a Lwa is when he/she arrives by riding on an attendee. This is usually the mambo or houngan who presides the religious service or ceremony. When this happens, the spirit will get the chance to communicate with those who are part of the ceremony. Here, the living may start presenting their requests and asking questions to the Lwa so they can take full advantage of the spirit's presence.

One fact about the Lwas you should know is that they showcase unique and distinctive behavior that makes them easily recognizable. Many even have specific actions and phrases you can immediately relate to them.

Once a Lwa gains recognition, the symbol dedicated explicitly to him will finally be given. For instance, there is this Lwa known as Erzulie Freda, who will only accept pink champagne. As for Papa Legba, the perfect gifts would be his cane, pipe, and straw.

The Three Main Families of Lwa

As indicated earlier, Voodoo practitioners must serve and worship a pantheon of spirits known as the Lwa. In modern Voodoo, the Lwa of the spirits practitioners communicate their concerns to and regularly interact with are categorized into three major families/nations – the Rada, Petro, and the Ghede. Let's get to know more about each family and the spirits or Lwas belonging to each one.

Rada Lwa Spirits

This family originated from Africa. It encompasses the deities and spirits that the slaves (taken to the New World) honored and respected, so they were the original Lwas. They turned into the primary spirits in the newly synthesized religion there. Most spirits who belong in this family are creative and benevolent. They are also primarily water spirits, which is why you can often see them served with water.

The Rada Lwa spirits are also recognized for their calm nature because they are less aggressive than the spirits and deities belonging to the Petro family. When serving Rada Lwas, it is crucial to remember that the most appropriate color is white. They also have stable personalities and are more likely to display a more defensive stance than an aggressive one.

Among the most prominent spirits or Lwas in the Rada family are:

Papa Legba

The Voodoo religion views Papa Legba as its most important Lwa. Associated with crossroads, he acts as the gatekeeper, making it possible for Voodoo devotees and practitioners to interact and communicate with the spirit. As the crossroad deity, he has full control over the gate between the world of the living and the spiritual world.

Not surprisingly, people perceive him as the counterpart of St. Peter in Roman Catholic. Papa Legba has a strong connection with stray dogs and appears like an older man holding crutches. His symbols, therefore, include stray dogs, tobacco and pipe, and spiritual crossroads.

The most appropriate offerings for him are rum, tobacco, spiced chicken, and black-eyed peas. You may also want to offer sacrificial animals to him, mainly goats and roosters.

Loko

Perceived as the patron of plants and healers, particularly the trees in Voodoo, Loko has a strong connection with the trees. He is the guardian of sanctuaries and the spirit of vegetation. He is capable of providing healing properties to leaves. Considered by many as the healing god, he is also a patron of most herb doctors. They often invoke this spirit whenever they need to undertake a treatment. They often put their offerings to him in a straw bag then hang them in the branches.

One recognizable feature of Loko is the stick that his hand carries. You can also recognize him through the pipe that his servant smoked. He likes the colors white and red the most.

Therefore, some of the animal offerings appropriate for this spirit are white or black goats and russet-colored oxen.

Many also recognize Loko because of his excellent judgment. With that, it is no longer surprising to see him being called in to act as a judge whenever there are conflicts. He does not tolerate injustice. He can transform into the wind then listen to the living without their knowledge. His primary duties, though, will always be on wood and forest vegetation.

Agwe

Agwe is also another famous Rada Lwa who is identified as the water spirit. With his water representation, it is no longer surprising to see seafarers interested in this Lwa. When performing ceremonies for him, it is advisable to do it close to the water. Some offerings that please him are white sheep, rum, gunfire, toy ships, and champagne.

You offer him these gifts by letting them float on the surface of the water. If the gifts or offerings go back to the shore, it means that Agwe refused them. As for the colors, the ones that represent him are usually white and blue. This Lwa is also linked to the Roman Catholic saint known as St. Ulrich. The reason is that St. Ulrich was seen holding a fish, so he has a strong connection with water.

Damballah-Wedo

Damballah-Wedo is also another of the most crucial Lwas, particularly in New Orleans Voodoo and Haitian Vodou. This spirit has a strong connection with the act of creation as he was also the one who offered help to Bondye in creating the cosmos. Portrayed by a snake or giant serpent, you will notice him displaying the behavior of a snake whenever he possesses a human. This means that he does a lot of whistling and hissing instead of talking.

The coils of Damballah-Wedo, though, played a crucial role in shaping the earth and heavens. He holds a lot of healing magic, wisdom, and knowledge. He can move the sea and land and holds the constant force representing life's venerations. As a creator, he is known for being a loving father to everything he created.

The mere presence of this Lwa is enough to bring harmony and peace. He is a primary source of life with a strong connection with rain and water. There are a couple of saints linked to him in the Roman Catholic religion – one of which is St. Patrick, the one who had successfully driven the snakes away from Ireland.

Another prominent religious figure linked to him is Moses, with his staff transformed to a snake to prove how powerful God was. He likes the color white. As for the offerings, you can gift Damballah-Wedo with corn syrup, eggs mounted on top of flour, white objects, like white flowers, and chicken.

Erzulie Freda

This Rada Lwa is recognized as the mistress ruling the realms of wealth and love. Voodoo practitioners and devotees may call or petition this Lwa to change their present financial conditions or add romance to their life. Take note, though, that the love that Erzulie brings does not usually last. The reason is that she tends to focus more on the brief yet erotic and passionate affairs of the ones seeking her help.

Erzulie Freda is also known for her passion, capriciousness, volatility, and flirtatious nature. The colors representing her include light blue and pink. Offerings she loves include flowers, white doves, perfume, sweet cakes, and champagne.

One thing to note about Erzulie is that she cries whenever she successfully possesses a devotee or practitioner during a ceremony or ritual because she often ends up unsatisfied with even the most luxurious items offered to her. She is the counterpart of Mater Dolorosa in the Roman Catholic faith.

Petro Lwa Spirits

The spirits or Lwas in the Petro family came from the New World, more specifically from modern Haiti. However, you can't find the Lwas or spirits here in the practice of African Vodou.

Usually, this family consists of spirits naturally more aggressive compared to other families. They also are fiery and warlike. The spirits here also have darker personalities than Rada's, but you can't categorize the two families into good and evil right away. If you do that, then there is a risk of misrepresentation, causing the rituals designed for offering assistance or causing harm to involve just one of them.

Instead, remember that even Rada Lwas, who seem to be all-white and pure, also have Petro counterparts in them. This means they also have their aggressive and dark side, though not as imminent as the ones in Petro. In other words, while Rada spirits are often perceived as benign or peaceful, they can also make evil magic.

Petro spirits, on the other hand, despite their aggressive nature, also perform beneficial workings such as healing. However, you can accurately call both families hot and cool, respectively.

To get to know more about this family, here are the most recognized Lwas/spirits under Petro:

Erzulie Dantor

Erzulie Dantor is the Petro side of Erzulie Freda. She is a vengeful and fiery spirit who came to life when practitioners struggled for independence. Many Voodoo practitioners invoke her to punish a lover who abused their partner or anyone who caused serious harm to their children.

Despite her harsh and wild nature, she still acts as a mother, a perfect one at that who genuinely cares for and watches her children. She is a disciplinarian and does not tolerate bad behaviors in children. Depicted as a loving and protective mother, you can associate her with Our Lady of Mt. Carmel, Our Lady of Perpetual Help, and Our Lady of Lourdes. All of them are recognized in the Catholic religion.

One offering she will most likely accept is *kleren*, which refers to a fiery drink in a rum infused with hot peppers. She also likes to receive peas and rice as gifts. As for the animal you can offer to her as a sacrifice, the best one would be a wild Creole pig. She also likes everything that's either blood red or navy blue.

Marinette

Another Lwa under the Petro family is Marinette. She is a Lwa of violence and power recognized in Haitian Vodou. Among all the Voodoo Lwas, she is considered the most dreaded one considering how powerful and cruel she is. The werewolves respect her. She does not like it when people burn humans and animals. These situations trigger her to become cruel, though she only shows her cruelty whenever she hates someone.

Another fact about Marinette you should know is that worshipping her is not a widespread practice in Haiti, though you can see her popularity rapidly growing in Southern areas. Her devotees hold ceremonies for her under a tent. It involves lighting it up with a big fire and throwing petrol and salt into the fire.

The ceremonial colors intended for Marinette include black and bloody red. She also likes it when Voodoo practitioners offer black roosters and black pigs plucked alive during ceremonies.

Met Kalfu

Met Kalfu has traits and aspects opposite of Papa Legba. He also has control of the crossroads and is capable of granting or denying your access to other spirits or Lwas. Moreover, he allows bad luck, injustices, misfortunes, and deliberate destructions to cross. He is also linked to almost all evil forces existing in the world.

Many even consider Met Kalfu as a trickster and a life destroyer. With his negative reputation, he may not be the perfect spirit to seek help from at first. It would be much better to approach the Lwas in Rada before approaching anyone from the Petro family. So, Met Kalfu is not the most suitable spirit for any witch to call on or summon haphazardly.

The bad reputation of Met Kalfu, combined with his being the dark version of Papa Legba, is why he is usually syncretized with Satan. He favors the color red and loves offerings in the form of rum infused with gunpowder.

Ghede Lwa Spirits

The third family consisting of Lwas is known as Ghede. The spirits belonging to this family are the unremembered and unclaimed dead. Besides representing the dead spirits, it also symbolizes the process of death itself, which all Voodooists believe is a simple passage or transition from one state to another. This means that death is a scenario they should not fear.

As a family, the spirits under Ghede are considered rude and loud. The spirits here also transport the souls of the dead. They have irreverent behaviors and are usually the ones who make sexual or obscene jokes. They also do dances following the act of sexual intercourse. Aside from that, Ghede Lwas or spirits can celebrate life even if someone is already close to death. The traditional colors of this family include purple and black.

Baron Samedi

He is one of the most prominent figures in the Voodoo religion. He is so prominent and influential that he leads the Guede family. He is the Lwa representing resurrection, gravestones, and graveyards. This spirit is usually chaotic and enjoys communicating with people. He also loves to smoke and drink.

One crucial fact about his personality you should know is that he is naturally morbid. He is wild, rowdy, and loud and loves to have a good time. Even if he drinks a lot and has an immense party lifestyle, this Ghede family leader still acts with style and class. He even guards and protects the dead.

Bardon Samedi is the counterpart of St. Martin de Porres. He is fond of the colors white, purple, and black. He likes to accept the gifts of rum, grilled peanuts, bread, cigars, and black coffee. Besides being the master of those already dead, Baron Samedi also acts as the giver of life. He is also the husband of Maman Brigitte.

Maman Brigitte

For those who practice the New Orleans Voodoo and the Haitian Vodoun religion, Maman Brigette is a prominent Lwa. She is strongly connected with cemeteries and death, but many also view her as the primary spirit of motherhood and fertility. She is also an extremely important Lwa as she absorbs the beliefs of other cultures into Voodoo.

She is also a strong representation of the ideal female in the religion. Despite her motherly nature, Maman Brigitte is known for being protective, strong, and aggressive to where she can punish anyone who does not respect the dead. She punishes anyone who does not provide the dead with a proper burial.

Most practitioners and devotees of Voodoo also invoke her for luck whenever they gamble. Her favorite ceremonial colors are purple and black. As for the offerings, among her favorites are black roosters, rum infused with pepper, and candles. Mary Magdalen is her counterpart in the Roman Catholic religion as they have a few similarities as far as their image is concerned.

The Mystic Marriage (Maryaj Mistik)

One more aspect about Lwas you have to learn involves the mystic marriage (Maryaj Mistik). It is an important aspect of the Lwas as it is a common occurrence among Vodou adherents, despite whether they have already undergone initiation. It happens as part of the ritual called the mystic marriage.

The entire ritual resembles an actual wedding ceremony conducted for two humans. This means it also requires the use of special attire and the presence of a priest, wedding ring, and wedding cake. The main goal of performing the mystic marriage is to build a special relationship with a Lwa, which is said to help in gaining more spiritual protection from them.

A taboo linked to this specific kind of marriage is the requirement to abstain from sex on any holiday-related to the Lwa. This is necessary to ensure that the practitioner or devotee to whom the Lwa gets married continues to receive the messages from their spiritual spouse. Such messages are often sent through dreams during the specific night when abstinence is a requirement.

Usually, practitioners or devotees choose to get married to their mèt tèt. This is the Lwa identified to walk with this person, whether or not through spiritual consultation or divination. In most cases, the devotee and their mèt tèt have a strong resemblance as far as their personalities are concerned. For instance, if you have Erzulie Freda as your mèt tèt, you can also have her personality, including being frivolous and generous.

Chapter 3: Becoming a Vodouisant

To become a Voodooist or just learn their ways, then you should understand the shared beliefs of those who practice it. You have already had a glimpse of these beliefs in the first couple of chapters, but it is time to dig a little deeper. That way, you will know exactly how Voodoo is practiced and how you can do it independently.

The Truth About Voodoo

Unlike the beliefs of many, the Voodoo community is not around to create zombies, summon evil spirits, and kill chickens and other animals for no reason. The Voodoo, necromantic, and nature spells are often done by Voodoo practitioners to serve, interact, and communicate with the powerful Lwas or spirits.

Similar to the Wicca religion, Voodoo is somewhat misunderstood. Several traditions and beliefs in Wicca and the Judeo-Christian faith are also part of the Voodoo community. With that in mind, Voodoo practitioners believe in celebrating important life events, such as births, deaths, and marriages. Those who are part of the Voodoo community believe in spirits (Lwas), and just one chief or supreme God also makes it resemble Christianity.

They also have their versions of priests and priestesses who contact Lwas whenever they perform long rituals. They are often the ones possessed or ridden by the spirits. Even if this form of possession has nothing to do with black magic, the untrained and unfamiliar may still look at it as an unsettling experience. So, only try to do complicated Voodoo spells once you have learned the most important facts and aspects.

The Birth of Misconceptions

It is no longer a secret; there are a lot of misconceptions revolving around Voodoo. Most of these misconceptions originated from the book written by Sir Spenser St. John in 1884 entitled Hayti: or the Black Republic. It inaccurately described Voodoo, demonstrating it as an evil religion involving wicked acts like cannibalism and human sacrifices.

The way Voodoo was described and depicted in the book is terrifying that those who were not part of this community started to fear it. It caused misunderstandings about Voodoo to spread from that moment – and even up to today. The fear and misconceptions further increased as Hollywood also depicted and cast Voodoo in a bad and unfavorable light.

Voodoo Beliefs and Christianity

The roots of Voodoo in Western Africa came from the ancient practices linked to animism and ancestor worship. This means they strongly believed that spirits could inhabit all things, such as plants and animals.

As has been indicated earlier, the practitioners and devotees of this religion also have strong faith in Bondye, the all-powerful and supreme God who stays detached from the affairs of humans.

Because of this God's detachment from humans, it has been the habit of practitioners to find help from their ancestors' spirits and the spirits of nature so they can find solutions to their problems.

Voodooists also believe that Lwas and humans have reciprocal relationships. They offer food and other possible gifts that the Lwa they are planning to reach out to will find appealing - so they can receive the spirit's help or assistance in return. During rituals, Lwas are often encouraged to possess believers and devotees present, allowing them to interact directly with the spirits.

Based on the community's beliefs, Voodoo and the Roman Catholic religions have a few similarities. Both religions are similar in the sense that their individual practitioners and devotees believe in:

- One Supreme Being
- The afterlife
- Ceremonies that require the consumption of body and blood
- Demons and evil spirits

Aside from that, Voodoos also believe in a *met tet*, which means master of the head. You can access this met tet within a Lwa. When compared to Christianity, the met tet is the counterpart of the patron saint. Lwas also resemble the saints in Christianity as they were once recognized as people who lived extraordinary and incredible lives. Like saints, deities also hold the unique attributes and responsibilities that all living beings should strive to follow.

The Lwas are also different from the saints in the Roman Catholic religion because some can be categorized as evil. For instance, there is an evil spirit in the Voodoo religion known as Baka, who can transform into an animal. Another evil Lwa (or spirit) in Voodoo is Kalfu, who controls the spiritual world's evil forces while also being closely linked to black magic.

Though, most spirits in Voodoo are good, which is why their attributes are shared with Christian saints. Voodoo practitioners also believe in Vilokan, the home of not only Lwas but also the deceased. This home is portrayed as a forested and submerged island with Papa Legba as its guard and protector. He is the one that the practitioners should appease before they can directly talk to any of the residents in the Vilokan.

Rituals and Practices

Voodoo practitioners also strongly believe in the importance of regularly ritualizing to communicate with the spirits. In most cases, the rituals include these practices:

- **Animal Sacrifices** - As the name suggests, it involves sacrificing animals during the Voodoo rituals. Various animals may be killed and then offered; the sacrifices offered will greatly depend on the specific Lwa practitioners plan to address. These offerings aim to provide spiritual sustenance to the Lwa. The flesh of the offered animals, on the other hand, is usually cooked then eaten during the ritual by those who participated in it.

- **Veves** - The rituals also include the use of drawings displaying the specific symbols representing the Lwa. These symbols are referred to in the community as veves. All Lwas have their individual veves or symbols that the practitioners have to draw - or use to worship or summon the spirits.

- **Voodoo Dolls** - Most Voodooists also believe in the significant role played by Voodoo dolls during rituals. You should note that the usual perception of Voodoo practitioners poking pins into these dolls is not reflective of the traditional religion. What the practitioners and devotees do, instead, is dedicate these Voodoo dolls to a specific Lwa. They also use dolls to attract the influence of the spirit.

The rituals that every Voodooist does also often revolve around interacting with the Lwa. The ceremonies make use of the veves along with songs, dancing, drumming, and praying. They believe in the need to gather together to serve and commune with the Lwa. In most cases, the ceremonies they set for a specific Lwa also correspond with a Roman Catholic saint's feast day, particularly the saint to whom the Lwa is connected.

Aside from that, all Voodoo practitioners must master all forms of ritual. They have to constantly remind themselves of the primary purposes of rituals - one of which is healing things or *echofe*, which is the actual term used for this purpose in Voodoo. This means it aims to change something, whether facilitating the healing process or eliminating any barriers.

Another important belief in Voodoo as for performing rituals is the need to practice secrecy. Before the later parts of the 20th century, devotees practiced this religion secretly.

The Soul

The Voodoo community also ingrains into the minds of its devotees and practitioners that a soul exists. This soul comes in two parts. The first one is the little good angel (ti bon ange), which refers to the conscience that makes one criticize and reflect on himself. The second one is the big, good angel (gros bon ange), which constitutes many vital aspects of a person, including his psyche, personhood, intelligence, and memory source.

Voodooists strongly believe these two essential parts of the soul live in one's head. The gros bon ange is also said to be capable of leaving your head and traveling even if you are sleeping or whenever a Lwa possesses you during a ceremony or ritual. According to Voodoo followers, there is a great chance for this specific part of your soul to get damaged. It may also be captured and attacked by evil magic at a time when it is no longer part of your body.

The two parts of the soul that the Voodooists believe in differ from the Catholic faith. The reason is that Roman Catholics believe there is only one soul. Despite that, the two religions continue to be the same because their beliefs include the possibility of evil possession. Both even perform an exorcism to eradicate the demon or evil person who entered or possessed someone.

Another important thing that the Voodooists believe regarding the soul is that the dead's spirits differ from the Guédé, whom they call Lwa. What makes them different is that the dead has to continue participating in the affairs of humans, particularly those who need sacrifices.

This specific belief makes it different from Christianity. Voodoo does not tell its practitioners there is an afterlife, which is part of Christians' beliefs regarding Heaven and Hell. In the Voodoo religion, the dead's spirits complain about being in a damp and cold realm that also causes them to experience hunger.

The Priests (Houngan) and Priestesses (Mambo)

Like other religions, mainly Roman Catholic, the Voodoo community also has its version of the priests. Called houngan or oungan in the community, the male priests serve as the dominating figures in Voodoo. They also have female counterparts (the priestesses) known as mambo or manbo. Based on numbers, rural Haitian Vodou is dominated by the Houngan. But the urban areas seem to have an equal balance between the Houngan and mambo (priests and priestesses).

These dominant figures in the Voodoo community play a lot of essential roles – among which are:

- Organizing liturgies
- Using divination for client consultations

- Preparing initiation rituals
- Creating healing remedies for the sick

The Lwa itself determines those who can become a priest or priestess in Voodoo. According to the community's beliefs, the person destined to become either a houngan or mambo will just receive a calling from Lwa. If one gets the calling, he/she should avoid refusing it. The reason is that any refusal from the calling to become a priest or priestess can cause misfortune.

Voodoo practitioners believe that the houngan's roles resemble the ones represented by Loco, one of the most recognized Lwas. Loco, together with Ayizan, his consort, was the first to hold the titles houngan and mambo in the community, making them the first two sources of knowledge to the community.

As Voodoo's dominating figures, the houngan and mambo also need to demonstrate their clairvoyance or their second sight. It is a gift from the supreme creator, which the community members can only access through dreams or visions. These figures derived their primary income from the community services (for example, healing the sick and selling amulets and talismans they created themselves). This also means that the competition between them was a bit stiff.

There are even instances when they become richer than the people or clients they serve. Still, they continue to be among the most well-respected and influential members of the Voodoo community. Without them, Voodoo will cease to exist. With these priests and priestesses, the community's faith also revolves around two fundamentals: life has no accidents, and all things are connected.

It is similar to the beliefs of other religious sectors that humans are not independent and separate. They are part of a vast community with strong connections to each other. The priests here also teach Voodoo practitioners about the golden rule in life: avoid doing to others what you do not want to be done to you.

The Voodoo Temples (Hounfo)

The *Hounfo* (or Voodoo temples) are also among the aspects of the community that the devotees firmly have faith in. This temple is the heart of most of their communal activities since this is where they undertake them. Note, though, that you can't find a single, uniform structure for this temple. Each varies in shape and size. You can find simple and basic shacks and more luxurious and lavish structures. The lavish ones are usually those that are in Port au Prince.

One thing to note about Hounfo or the Voodoo temples is that each has a unique design, greatly dependent on the taste and available resources of the priest or priestess running it. Each temple is also independent and unique so that you can see its unique customs and traditions.

In the Hounfo or temple, you will find the peristyle, which is considered the main space where the ceremonies occur. Here, you will find posts constructed from corrugated iron, with bright paintings, and these are used in holding up the roof. One post, specifically located at the center, is called the poto mitan, the one used as a pivot whenever they do ritual dances. The spirits or Lwas also pass through it every time there is a ceremony for them.

The Voodoo temple is also noticeable by the many sacred objects surrounding it. Here, you can find sacred items, like a black cross, iron bar, and pool of water. There are also sacred trees used to mark the temple's external boundary. A Hounfo with these sacred trees surrounding it also comes with other holy items hanging in them, including animal skulls and some strips of material.

You can also find different kinds of animals, including birds and a few mammals, like goats, inside the Hounfo's perimeters. The primary purpose of having these animals is to keep them handy whenever they need to use them for sacrifices during rituals.

The people gathering at the temple are the actual members of the spiritual group or community who seriously practice and believe in Voodoo. These members are called the children of the house or the pititt-caye. They worship the spirits in the temple using various forms of ritual and through the supervision and authority of the priests or houngan and the priestesses or mambo.

There is also what is called the *ounsi* in the community. It refers to those who are committed to offering their service to the Lwa for their entire lives. Males and females of the community can be an ounsi, but most are typically female. They hold several duties and responsibilities: offering animal sacrifices, participating in dances that require them to be fully prepared for the possible possession of a Lwa and keeping the peristyle clean.

For a Voodoo community member to become an ounsi, he/she has to go through the imitation ceremonies that the priests and priestesses will conduct. Here, the priests and priestesses will oversee and facilitate the entire training process. They also serve as healers, protectors, and counselors for the aspiring ounsi. With the many roles that they have to play to make the goal of the ounsi come to life, the latter must show their respect and obedience to the former in return.

An ounsi will also be tasked to act as the choir mistress or the hungenikon. The one assigned to this role will play the vital task of supervising the singing of the liturgy. He/she will also need to control the ceremony's rhythm helped by a cha-cha rattle that needs to be shaken constantly.

Another relevant figure in the group of ounsi is the confidant or *confiance*. This ounsi will be the one to supervise the administrative functions of the Voodoo temple (Hounfo). The ones initiated by the priests and priestesses will also be required to build or form families within the community.

Anyone interested in becoming part of the Voodoo community can participate in a specific Hounfo if it is present in the locality where he resides. If you have a relative who is already a community member, you can be part of the congregation, too. Suppose you want to offer your service on a specific Lwa. There, you can also find Voodoo temples devoted to such a spirit. It is also possible to be part of the congregation where the priest or priestess has left a good impression on you.

The Initiation Rituals

Now it is time to know more about the initiation rituals you have to go through to become a Voodooist or a Voodoo devotee or practitioner yourself.

One crucial fact to remember is that there is a particular hierarchy in this community, which requires potential members to undergo a set of initiation rituals. Basically, it has multiple levels – the last of which allows one to hold the highest rank in the community, the houngan (priest) or mambo (priestess).

The initiation is usually a long process, mostly taking a couple of weeks. Basically, you must go through the initial rite, known as *kanzo*, first. Here, your main responsibility would be to participate in the first few ceremonies called *bat ge*, which means the act of beating a war. You will most likely encounter this during the initiation since you will be winning a battle to ensure that the aspiring voodooists will gain possession of the mysteries.

Each temple differs based on the number of nights they often spend performing the bat ge. Regardless of that number, the ritual's focus will usually be on a unique and distinctive Petro-based altar called a *bila*. One night of bat ge will also be dedicated to a ceremony called *pile fey*, which involves crushing herbs.

The crushed herbs will be used over the entire duration of the kanzo. You can expect these herbs to be empowered and charged specifically through the special ceremony. There will also be one night specifically dedicated to initiating the tie packets. This ceremony will require the participation of only the houngans and mambos.

After that, a series of special baths symbolizing the death of those intending to become voodooists will occur. Various Voodoo temples and houses differ in the number of days or times they perform these baths. Some do it for three days, while others complete the process within just one to two days. The number of baths that a candidate must take may differ based on the temple or house he is in.

As for the actual process, expect the candidate to be led in a procession first to reach the priest or priestess who will be the one to bathe them. Once done, he can rest for a bit while waiting for the following procedure he has to go through. The Kouche kanzo refers to secluding the initiate that may also involve a lot of dancing.

As part of the initiates, you will also need to feed Ayizan with sacred food. The whole ritual also involves setting up a special and distinctive throne for Ayizan. Here, you can expect Ayizan to show up occasionally by possessing someone. His presence will focus more on blessing the initiates. After that, you and the other initiates must remain secluded while doing certain activities that should not be revealed to anyone.

You must remain in seclusion for up to a week or seven days. Once you have completed that, expect to come out as a renewed, empowered, and strengthened version of yourself. You may even be reborn as someone new. It could be as a houngan, mambo, or a *hounsis*.

Before leaving your exact seclusion area, you must go through another ceremony called *brule kanzo*. Here, you will hold boiling cornmeal while being tested for your ability to handle fire. This activity is important, as it will serve as proof you are indeed strong.

When it is time to leave, you will be led on a procession once again while wearing white clothes and straw hats. You will be baptized as part of the community in the evening, followed by a party to honor your successful initiation and baptism.

Your successful completion of the seclusion period is your means of entry to the congregation and the entire community. The last stage of the whole initiation process will most likely involve you receiving a rattle. A Lwa may also possess you, as the new initiate, for the first time, which will mark the end of the initiation process.

Should You Become an Initiate?

If you feel like being an initiate is your calling, then you should give it a go. Consider going through the entire initiation process so you can finally become a full-fledged voodooist. One thing to remember, though, is that not all people are fit for it. Not everyone finds the entire process desirable and is genuinely willing to handle the actual initiation's responsibilities.

Despite that, successful initiation comes with many rewards, though it also requires you to carry many responsibilities. Even if you are not born into this religion, you can still be a Voodooist if you want to be by approaching the right people in the community.

Communicate with a renowned and responsible houngan or mambo as much as possible. With their help, you can be initiated to be a Voodooist, hounsi, or even a houngan or mambo. Just get in touch with the most reputable community members who can invite you to the initiation after getting to know you and your potential.

Remember that being successfully accepted to the community somewhat resembles adoption or marriage if you decide to undergo the initiation. In other words, you will become a full-fledged member of a family. With that in mind, make sure you will be genuinely happy with your prospective new family. You need to open yourself up to them so they can learn more about you and accept you.

Patience is also important. Note that the entire process will be long, but it is all worth it. The best way to handle it is to ask questions regarding prospective teachers and initiators. Assess their reputation and credentials, too. Observe the way they work personally and the things they say whenever they communicate with others. If you plan to learn from a houngan or mambo, choose one with a verifiable and solid training and initiatory history.

Pick someone who is mature and has a lot of experience. You may have a challenging experience finding the right person to teach and train you during the initiation. Still, with patience and the constant seeking of guidance from your ancestors and spirits, you will ultimately find what you are looking for.

Chapter 4: Voodoo Veves

Now, we will talk about the symbols or veves used in the Voodoo community. All Voodoo religion practitioners refer to the veves as drawings capable of representing or symbolizing the deities and the Lwas or spirits they worship.

Unlike other religions and traditions that use pictures and statues to symbolize their worshiped gods, the Voodoo community members are recognized for using veves or Voodoo symbols whenever their ceremonies occur. The Haitian Vodou tradition, for instance, is recognized for using various powders in tracing at least one esoteric sigil to represent every Lwa.

A Closer Look at Veves

If you are not familiar with veves, the best way to describe them would be astral and spiritual scripts used to communicate with the Lwas or spirits. You can't consider them as stylized symbols that refer to complex iconographies. Instead, these veves are alphabets composing mystical phrases meant to summarize any metaphysical concepts, promoting ease in understanding them.

Besides the Voodoo symbols that characterize different Lwas, several other crucial elements appear in them. You must insert these additional crucial elements to provide more meaning or produce a more dynamic action to every accessible spiritual current.

As part of the Voodoo tradition, practitioners appeal to the Lwas or spirits and invite them to possess or ride human bodies. This is the only way to interact or communicate with them directly. With that, expect Voodoo rituals and ceremonies to involve a lot of dancing, chanting, music, and drumming. Besides all the mentioned practices, the participants must draw Voodoo symbols called veves.

These Voodoo symbols are important because they also appeal to certain Lwas, similar to how certain colors, chants, drumbeats, and objects do. You can't just draw any veve in a ritual or ceremony, though. Note you have to draw a symbol depending on the specific Lwa called upon in the ceremony.

Usually, drawing the symbols should be done on the ground. You have to use sand, cornmeal, or any other powdery substance to draw the symbol then obliterate it during the ceremony. As the veve symbolizes the actual figures of astral forces, it is crucial when appealing to any Lwa. During every ceremony, you can take advantage of the veve to reproduce the astral forces it represents, which will oblige the Lwas to come down to the Earth.

Another important fact about the veve symbols and designs is that each varies based on the local customs and the actual names of the Lwas. Some of these veves also share a few elements and similarities. One example is Damballah-Wedo, who is known as a serpent deity. Because of that, you will notice his veve often incorporating a couple of snakes.

As intricate symbols of Voodoo spirits or Lwas, it is necessary to use these veves in rituals and ceremonies. You can liken these Voodoo symbols to the sigils often used when doing ritual magic. Each veve is a material representation of a particular Lwa. Each symbol is a magic point. With that in mind, it is no longer surprising to see animal sacrifices and food offerings being placed on the drawn veve of the Lwa.

Each Voodoo symbol or veve is also made to graphically reproduce a Lwa's attributes and their ritual signs. Note that all Lwas have their own complex symbols or veves that the practitioners must trace on the ground before a ritual. This is done using a powdered eggshell or any other similar substance.

Anyone initiated to be part of the Voodoo tradition needs to be capable of drawing the veve correctly. The reason is this symbol will become even more powerful if you draw it using the right and accurate details.

Most Important Veves in the Voodoo Community

With the numerous Lwas and spirits in the Voodoo religion, it is safe to say there are literally hundreds of veves you can use for any ritual or ceremony. However, out of these many veves, a few seem to be used more often, making them extremely important in all devotees and practitioners' lives. Some of the most important veves in this religion include:

Veve of Aizan

Aizan is recognized as the spirit or Lwa presiding over initiation rituals. She has such power because she, herself, is a mambo. The veve specifically used for this spirit is a couple of intertwined Vs. It refers to the primitive androgyne's V, which also features branches that have horns on their ends. You can see in the symbol a diamond in the center, which looks like a palm tree leaf with leaves.

The name of Ayizan means sacred earth. This name was also derived from the term, Aïzan, a Fon language, which means earthen mounds piling up the marketplace as a means of honoring primal ancestors. Her name was also derived from Azan, a relevant term, which means palm frond fringes that one can use in demarcating a sacred space. These origins of her name are why this Lwa holds a particular veve, with palm frond being her primary symbol.

Ayizan is also known for being the first or archetypal priestess or mambo, which is why she is often connected to priestly mystery and knowledge, including those related to the natural world and the initiation rites for any aspiring Voodoist.

As the Lwa of commerce and marketplace, you can call her to protect doors, entrances, barriers, gateways, public spaces, and markets. She can cleanse and purify a place and create a sacred space. The saint whom she is syncretized to in the Catholic Church is St. Claire.

Veve of Papa Legba

Papa Legba is probably the oldest and most vital Lwa or spirit in the Voodoo community. Many consider him the Lwa of entryways, doors, paths, gates, crossroads, trickery, and sorcery. He plays such an important role in the Voodoo community in the sense that other spirits or Lwas will not get to the Earth without his permission.

As he holds the keys for both humans and Lwas to interact, you can see him being identified with the famous Catholic saint, St. Peter. Just like St. Peter, Papa Legba also acts as a strong foundation for the religion. Papa Legba's veve or Voodoo symbol features a cross with equal sides. This makes him strongly connected to the cross, which is why many Voodooists perceive Papa Legba as the community's Christ.

Since he is also the master of crossroads, you can see Papa Legba governing sorcery. He is even considered the greatest magician ever introduced. Papa Legba is also considered by the Voodoo community as the sun, an element worshipped by practitioners as a force that gives life. Perceived as the sun, Papa Legba also represents the East and the orient, the specific place where it is possible to control magic and create life.

This transformed him into the God of creation. The cardinal point you can see in the magical cross in his symbol is the East. This makes it crucial for him to be greeted first whenever he welcomes spirits or Lwas. It will be easier for him to open the doors, allowing other spirits to enter.

As the master of highways and guardian of crossroads, you can also see Papa Legba having crossroads as part of his symbolisms. These crossroads represent the union of vertical and horizontal astral forces, making it possible for Papa Legba to control the spirit or the God's astral-causal magic.

Drawings representing Papa Legba also perceive him as an old man. Voodooists relate him to water bearers. The reason is that he also has full control of the Earth's fluid, particularly circulation and blood. Moreover, he represents bones, bone marrow, and vertebrae. You can see these items being symbolized by a central post known for being the peristyle's backbone.

Veve of Agwe

Agwe, the spirit ruling the fish, aquatic plants, and the sea, is the patron Lwa of all the sailors and fishermen in the Voodoo community, particularly those in Haiti. Many invoke him using the names tadpole of the pond and seashell. Under Agwe's influence, it is possible to witness many flora and fauna in the sea. You can also find many boats sailing in the sea because of his influence, which is why a boat is part of his veve or Voodoo symbol.

The veve of Agwe features brightly painted boats. These boats could also be shells or oars. There are also instances when small metal fish are used in place of the boat symbol. It is crucial to note that the process of serving Agwe differs from when calling other spirits or Lwas. The reason is that Agwe, himself, can also be seen in the sea.

With that in mind, you can see many Voodooists using actual shells, besides the Voodoo symbol they draw for him when summoning or invoking him, during celebrations or rituals. You must welcome him with a towel and wet sponge whenever you see him coming out of the water because of the heat.

To worship or call upon him, it is often necessary to prepare a boat containing all the foods he favors (including savory and exotic foods), and other things he likes, including champagne, naval rum, toy ships, and gunfire. The siren of the sea, La Sirene, is known for being the female counterpart of Agwe. He is also the counterpart of St. Ulrich in the Roman Catholic religion.

Veve of Damballah-Vedo

Another veve that all members of the Voodoo community consider as extremely important is that of Damballah-Vedo. As the Lwa of snakes, serpents, rain, life, and water, you can see his Voodoo symbol or veve appearing like two prominent serpents. This veve reflects the fact that most Voodooists depict him as a snake or serpent.

He has a strong connection with the ancestors. Damballah-Vedo is also one of the wisest and oldest Lwas, together with his partner in creation, Ayida-Wedo. The fact that the entire creative process has to be shared by a man and woman is why his veve comes with two snakes or serpents instead of just one.

The important role played by Damballah-Vedo in the Voodoo community can never be underestimated. He is strongly linked to the process of creation, making him a prominent figure. Besides that, Damballah-Vedo is also recognized for his ability to bring harmony and peace.

Veve of Baron Samedi

Baron Samedi, the head of the Ghede family representing all dead and living souls, also has his own veve or Voodoo symbol. This symbol mainly has a cross, though this cross does not symbolize the one used by Christians or the Roman Catholics. What it symbolizes, instead, is a crossroad.

The reason could be that you can usually find Baron Samedi at the crossroads, specifically between the worlds of those already dead and the living. Part of his routine is digging graves for the dead and greeting their souls after burial. He will then lead these dead souls to the underworld.

You can also find two interlocking V's drawn vertically in the veve of Baron Samedi. These figures symbolize the union of two sexes considered as the major components of the primitive androgyne. The veve also features three degrees or steps, the one where the cross stands, and each step represents the level of initiation. The first step is a symbol of ordinary life, so you can see it being decorated by phalluses and working instruments.

The second step symbolizes the movement that the *acon* (a sacred rattle that a priest uses) traces in the air. The highest step or degree represents the secret held by the best among those who became priests. The one who holds this secret is also known for being gifted with double vision. Overall, this veve is so powerful that it illustrates the strong connection between death and the afterlife.

Veve of Ougon

Part of the Rada family is the spirit (Lwa) known as Ougon. The primary Voodoo symbols used for this Lwa include iron, palm frond, and a dog. These symbols or veves represent the significant role played by Ougon in terms of mediation, function, and transformation. The fact that iron is this spirit's main emblem or symbol is also why most ceremonies and altars dedicated to him use and display objects made of iron.

This means that aside from drawing the veve, you may also summon him by wearing chains with iron implements. Festivals honoring Ougon also usually display guns, knives, wrenches, scissors, blacksmith implements, and any other implements based on iron that most use in daily life. The Voodoo symbol of Ougon is also proof he is a deity (orisha) and spirit (Lwa) capable of presiding over things like iron, war, politics, and hunting.

Ougon is also recognized in the community as the god of intelligence, political power, pioneering, medicine, and justice. These can be connected to the symbol of the exact tool capable of advancing humans' mastery over the surrounding environment. In Africa, you can see Ougon being worshiped by many blacksmiths, with most originating from Yoruba. Ougon also favors alcohol and women.

Veve of Gran Bwa

Another Lwa who plays a huge role in the Voodoo community is Gran Bwa. A part of the Petro family, Gran Bwa strongly connects with magic, secrets, and healing. He can conceal specific items from the eyes of those who are not initiated in this religion. Many summon him during initiation ceremonies.

He is considered the master of Vilokan's forests because he is the reason behind his symbol or veve, which you can see as strongly linked to plants and trees. The name given to him, Gran Bwa, also means big tree, which is why his symbol also somewhat signifies this connection.

Aside from his strong connection with trees and plants, Gran Bwa also represents the practices linked to them, including herbalism. This spirit is also recognized as the master of the wilderness, so his personality includes unpredictability and wildness. Despite that, he also shows many great qualities, including being a fairly approachable and loving Lwa.

One specific object that Gran Bwa considers sacred is silk cotton or the mapou tree. This tree is a native of Haiti, which connects the spiritual and material worlds. You can often see mapou being represented by a central pole in Voodoo temples' courtyards. Gran Bwa also gained the recognition of being a protector and guardian of ancestors who travel from one world to the next all the time.

Veve of Erzulie Freda

Erzulie Freda is also a prominent Lwa in the Voodoo community, so her veve is popular. As the goddess of beauty and love, it is no longer surprising to see her veve coming with a squared heart at the center. This makes her Voodoo symbol more representative of romantic love, luxury, and sweetness. You can summon her whenever you feel like it is time to add more luxury and love to your life.

Each square and inner point found in this veve or symbol also symbolizes a force ready to explode. You can also see a voodoo star on top of it and two rising moons. You can find the quintessential sun spirit, which is a staff of Papa Legba. This indicates that uniting feminine and masculine principles is what results in love. It fuses and unites fire and water together.

Another thing you will notice in the veve of Erzulie Freda is the large loops on its sides. This represents balance, which means that there should be no prevailing principle. You can also see an inverted ram's horns in the veve, which signifies possession.

This could mean the desire of Erzulie Freda to get more from those who worship and follow her. Despite her wealth, she still finds the world disappointing and constantly reminds everyone that material things should not be the only wealth you can attain.

How to Draw Voodoo Symbols (Veves)

Now that you know some of the most commonly used veves or symbols in Voodoo, it is time to know more about how you can make one yourself. Note that veves serve as powerful tools you can use to connect with a higher energy and Voodoo magic, spirits, and deities.

You need to draw the veves on the ground using any powdery substance like sand and cornmeal. You then have to obliterate them during ceremonies and rituals. You have to trace the drawings manually on the ground before the start of a ritual or ceremony.

Besides sand and cornmeal, you can also use coffee powder, white flour, herbs, and brick powder for the purpose. Your choice will greatly depend on the specific division and mystery you intend to evoke. To scatter the powder, slide it between your thumb and middle and index fingers. Use the fingers on your right hand, so you can attain regular traces.

After tracing the veve, you have to spray it with a suitable libation. Put a candle at the center, then activate it by ringing either a maraca or bell. While doing so, recite prayers and invocations to the mystery of the multiple Lwas you intend to call, summon, or invoke.

If you perform a Voodoo service as a means of feeding a few Lwas simultaneously, then incorporate all their ritual emblems in the veve when drawing it. Make sure that all Lwas are part of your drawn symbol. This may cause the final symbol or veve to be complex while also covering a huge part of the peristyle.

It is possible to make the veve into a painting, screen-print, patchwork, banner, artwork, and wall hanging. However, take note it would be much better to handcraft or draw it yourself. Remember that it will become more powerful and effective in summoning Lwas and manifesting your heart's desires if you draw it manually.

When drawing the veve, it would also be much better to use both your hands. By doing that, the entire process will surely symbolize the pathways one has to take to get into the worlds of the invisible and visible. In most cases, this pathway is around the Poteau mitan or center pole. This spot forms a new conduit where the divine can easily travel.

Make sure that you also draw the symbol correctly. It is the key to summoning the correct Lwa. If you draw it incorrectly, then it will only lead to summoning shadows or malevolent spirits. An incorrectly drawn veve may also result in summoning the wrong Lwa, someone for whom the ritual or ceremony was not made.

Do not forget to bless the completed drawing of the veve with sacred waters, too. You can also use alcohol or rum for this purpose. Another important part of the ritual involves drawing a veve to summon a Lwa is dancing. It is crucial for those who participate in the ritual or ceremony to dance on the drawn veves barefoot.

This is essential to assist divine energies to penetrate their bodies, allowing spiritual possession to take place. It also contributes to the veve setting the stage for communicating and communing with the divine.

Using Veves in Talismans or Flags

Most of those who are already familiar with using talismans fully know how useful the symbols integrated into them are -especially when it comes to protecting themselves from evil and attracting fortune, or whatever their intention is. When planning to use these talismans, though, remember that the symbols required differ based on their origin.

If you are from the Voodoo community, then the symbols you have to integrate into the talismans should be the corresponding symbols in the religion, known as veves. These talismans include amulets, trinkets, jewelry pieces, or even a small flag you can use to keep yourself protected or draw positive things to you, like prosperity, money, love, and health.

Being sacred tools, you need to charge them using the waxing moon's power. They serve as magical tools capable of generating positive energies that can attract whatever you desire. To use veves in talismans, follow these basic steps:

• **Decide On the Reason You Need the Talisman** - Once you know your intention, conduct research on the seals, planets, and the specific spirits or Lwas linked to the things you intend to attract.

• **Collect Important and Useful Items, Like Bones, Stones, Herbs, and Crystals** - Ensure you pick those with a strong connection to your talisman's intended purpose. Your goal is to seek the help of the intended spirit to determine what you think is right and appropriate.

• **Draw the Veve or Voodoo Symbol** - This is necessary to enchant your talisman. Ensure that you also write a message, which states the specific thing you want your talisman to do. Remove all vowels from the message. Remove every third letter of the words, then rearrange the remaining ones until an abstract image is formed, which differs from the original statement. After that, you can draw the veve or symbol in a cloth bag.

• **Build Your Ritual Space** - Ensure it contains everything needed for the ritual or ceremony. Among the things, you may need frankincense or sandalwood incense and white candles. These are often good tools you can use to set up your ritual space and make it as sacred as possible.

- **Choose to Do the Ritual When You Can Focus Intently** - Do it privately and when you are alone. If possible, pick a planetary hour or day, which corresponds to your talisman's main purpose.

- **Encircle Yourself With Lighted Candles** - Summon the gods and spirits you believe in when doing so. Also dedicate a few minutes to meditation. Ensure that you focus intently on the veve or symbol. Meditate based on your heart's desires. Stay away from all forms of distraction and communicate or interact with the related spirits.

- **Once Done, Hold the Talisman** - Recite your intentions or wishes when doing so.

During the last step, visualize the answers that your summoned Lwa or spirit may give you. Do it while the talisman continues to warm up with your body's heat. Feel the excitement of your intentions coming to life. Allow the energy to flow not only to your hands but also to the talisman.

Observe the talisman. Once you feel like it completely absorbed all the energy, you can use a gesture to seal it off. For instance, if you put the items inside a bag, you can seal them off by kissing them. Then feel joy once you notice your desire happening.

To use the talisman, you can wear it or put it in your room. Another way to use it is to put it inside a pouch and carry or wear it. Fortunately, you can also put it in a box and place it on your altar whenever you do not feel the need to wear it.

Should You Use Veve Tattoos?

Many people now decide to put tattoos of Voodoo symbols or veves on their bodies. This is a mistake, and you should avoid doing it at all costs. Remember that the veve is a Voodoo symbol primarily meant to be drawn on a floor or a sacred object during a ritual.

Each of these veves is linked to a specific spirit. It is drawn during a ceremony as a means of capturing the attention of a Lwa. That it is a sacred symbol to the Voodoo community makes it quite unpleasant to put it on your body. It should be used at the appropriate time and place. Putting it on your body in the form of a tattoo may invite unwanted effects and issues as it may lead to inviting negative energies and the wrong spirits.

Chapter 5: Build Your Voodoo Shrine

If you are serious about becoming a Voodoo practitioner and devotee, you have to learn how to build your own voodoo altar or shrine. It should be dedicated to the ancestor or Lwa you favor and want to summon all the time. It may be a daunting task, especially for those who are still beginners in this religion, but once you have everything ready, you can learn the basics and eventually master how to prepare and build your Voodoo shrine.

Types of Altars

The first step you have to take when building your Voodoo shrine or altar is to determine its exact purpose. This will show you the specific type of shrine or altar you have to build. It will guide you to determine the tools and objects you need and the requirements you have to adhere to, especially regarding the positioning and placement of the sacred items.

Here are the different types of altar or shrine you can build:

- **Ancestor Altar** – You can build this one if your goal is to connect with your ancestors. You will be putting pictures of your departed loved ones on the altar. You may also include some of their personal items, particularly those they love, to serve as their reminders. It is also advisable to put a plate and cup for food and drink offerings.

- **Deity Altar** – As the name suggests, this altar is meant to worship Lwas, spirits, and deities. You can make this altar a shared space but make sure that the specific spirits and deities you intend to summon permit it. For this altar to work, dedicate a space to leave your offerings. There should also be a space where you can light candles and incense and offer items that the spirit or deity favors. Sometimes, the altar holds idols as a means of standing in for the Lwas or spirits you intend to worship or honor in that space.

- **Nature Altar** – You can also dedicate a space designed to honor nature. In most cases, you can see these altars being filled with things representing the natural elements – among which are seashells and stones. Remember that the nature altar can't be used as a sacred space for your offerings.

- **Temporary Altar** – You can create this type of altar for certain events, like a festival meant to worship or honor a certain Lwa or deity. You can also use it whenever you need to do a certain magical rite. It is meant for rituals and holidays. That it is temporary means you can dismantle it right after the event.

The specific purpose you intend your altar to perform should be the deciding factor on the type you have to choose.

Finding the Appropriate Space

After deciding on the type of altar or shrine to build, the next thing you should do is to look for the right space where you can set it up. You need enough space so you can comfortably perform the ritual. Some things you can use as your altar or shrine would be:

- **A Small Table** - You may want to use your coffee or end table for your altar. One advantage is that you can easily move it, plus it provides a clean and flat surface capable of holding various things. You can also thrift it conveniently. Just make sure you spend time cleaning the table before using it.

- **The Top of Your Dresser** - If you have an unused dresser at home, then you can use the top for your sacred altar or shrine. It is a great idea, especially if you have kids and pets at home since they can't easily reach it. Since it is a dresser, you can put it in a place where people can see right away and interact or communicate every day. It may not be a suitable choice for you, though, if you are uncomfortable setting up your altar or shrine in your own room.

- **Cabinet** - You can also use any cabinet you can find at home. It provides adequate space, plus it comes with multiple levels, giving you the chance to pick a level for a specific purpose. If you have only a small space, then you can set aside a bit of space from a desk, bookshelf, or dresser in your home.

However, ensure that even if you're sharing a particular space, avoid allowing items that are not supposed to be in the altar to take the space dedicated for it.

Consider and prioritize privacy, too. Despite having a full closet to accommodate a huge setup for your altar, it will be hard to do your rituals or ceremonies if you display it out in the open. You can put a tiny altar in a closet, which you can close at any time.

Those are just a few examples of items of spaces that you can set aside for your altar or shrine. Remember that your choice serves as an external representation of inner mysteries. It tangibly shows what may happen in your spirits and hearts. This means you have to choose the most suitable space wisely.

Also, the shrine or altar you have built is the key for you to reflect, honor, remember, and heal from grief - anytime you want. It works as your private space - one that lets you reflect, grieve, meditate, honor, remember, and engage in personal rituals with anyone who has departed.

You can also use a small and portable shrine - one you can conveniently carry anywhere you want. It could be an extremely small one, like a matchbook, which can easily fit your pocket. You can also use a bigger one but that you can easily slip into your briefcase or purse.

By choosing a shrine you can carry anywhere, it will be easy for you to maintain the connection you have established with your loved one - even those who have died. It also gives you a sacred space you can use to remember someone or perform a personal ritual regardless of where you are.

What Do You Need for Your Voodoo Altar/Shrine?

Once you already have a space for your altar or shrine, it is time to gather the things necessary for you to make it work for your Voodoo rituals. You may want to put a few things on the altar, such as your magical tools. However, remember that the ultimate goal should be to make the altar as functional as possible. With that in mind, you have to set it up with items that will let you attain your goals.

Some things that include the altar are:

• *Symbols of four classical elements* – These elements are the earth, air, fire, and water. It is crucial to align these elements with the four corresponding cardinal directions. Here, you have to use a bowl containing sand or earth in your altar's north aspect to represent the earth, incense in the east to represent air, water in the west, and charcoal or candle in the south to symbolize fire.

• *Candles* – Your altar should also have candles. It could be a god candle or goddess candle, depending on what your ritual or spell requires. It would also be best to choose different colors for the candles. You may also use candles that represent the four directions. Just ensure that you also have a match or lighter so you can easily light them.

• *Wand* – You may also want to put a wand on your altar. This wand is often helpful in directing energy. Note that the specific manner through which you will be laying this wand and the exact spot where you will be putting it on the altar will greatly depend on what you intend to do, but wise advice is to put it close to or on the altar.

• *Athame* – You can also put an athame on your altar. It refers to a blunt and double-edged blade used in channeling energy. It often has a black handle and blunt blade, which helps prevent accidents during ceremonies and rituals. One thing you should remember about an athame is to prevent yourself from using it for physical cutting. What you have to do, instead, is use it for cutting energy symbolically. With the athame in your altar, you can guide energy every time you do your rituals or ceremonies.

• *An item that makes your shrine or altar unique from its surroundings* – If you set up the altar in a different spot, use a table cover or cloth. It should indicate that the entire space is dedicated to the Voodoo altar or shrine.

If you set it up in a shared space, like the top of your dresser or your work desk, then look for an item that will instantly send a warning that a particular space is only meant for the altar. By doing that, you can maintain the orderliness and cleanliness of that particular spot. It can also prevent you from placing other things that are not supposed to be on the altar.

One thing you can do is to create a small crate or box. It should serve as the shrine. You may also set it up as a tray where you can keep important things on.

• *A spot where you can put anything you want to offer to the Lwa or ancestor* – It could be a small dish or tray. Dedicate it to the offerings so you can easily monitor what you have left in there during the ritual.

• *A clear space where you can put temporary items* – There should be a clear space dedicated for some temporary items you need. It is advisable to put divinatory tools on your altar, so you can bless or charge them right away. Some examples would be certain icons designed to represent specific issues you feel require help. By dedicating a clear space for such a purpose, you can prevent the order of your altar from being untidy.

• *A personal item so valuable and meaningful to you* – You may want to put such things if you want your altar to have some personal effects. By putting something meaningful to you on your altar, you can easily create a channel between the actual practice and you. You may add a painting, idol, a specific incense, or anything that is personal to you and meets your specific needs.

Place any other item you think you need and have the available space for. You may also want to put any components of the spell you need, like ale and cakes. If you plan to use your altar to celebrate a particular event or holiday that specifically points to the Lwa you intend to summon, decorate your altar based on that, too. Ensure that the altar has everything you need to do your rituals effectively.

Building Your Altar

Once you have chosen the space, the things you need, and the actual altar you will be using, it is time for you to set it up. It is crucial to note that you can create the altar either for a public or private space. The only things you should never forget incorporating into this space are respect and sincerity. Ensure that you also build your altar based on these tips:

- Clean the surface first using a spiritual solution, such as rose water or Florida water. Wipe it dry, then pray aloud to express your desire to make the space and specific surface intended for the altar holy.

- If you are using a table constructed from wooden material, you can bless it using oil, such as ancestor or Van oil. After that, look for a cloth you can use to cover the altar. It is preferable to use white, but you can also be more creative in your cloth choice. Try avoiding synthetic materials and dark colors, though. It would be best to go for cotton then use it to cover the altar.

- Make sure to put beautiful and meaningful objects on the altar. They can be Voodoo dolls, statues, talismans, roots, stones, or flowers. Pick things that have special meaning or those that inspire you. The altar should also contain incense, candles, anointing oils, or perfumes.

- Put water on the altar. Another tip for setting up the perfect Voodoo altar or shrine is to regularly put water on it. It can contribute a lot to gaining more clarity in life. Do not forget to change the water frequently.

- Identify the exact purpose of the altar. You can make it to honor the dead or living, particularly those who have inspired you. If so, then ensure that you put pictures of them on the altar, too.

- Meditate before the shrine or altar you have built every day. This should serve as your daily ritual. When meditating, concentrate on the positive changes you intend to make happen in your life and in the lives of your family members, loved ones, and the entire Voodoo community.

In most cases, all Voodoo devotees, even priests, make it a point to build a small altar designed for a certain Lwa in their households. They use these altars or shrines as focal points for their meditation and prayer. It is at this altar or shrine that they perform private devotionals. This private home altar specifically designated for a Lwa is called an *ogantwa*.

This ogantwa holds many items found in hounfo's *badji* (temple room), such as lithographs or exact representations of the spirit or Lwa, satin scarves made of different colors, thunderstones, and dolls. You may also have to put a kind of perpetual lamp here. You can also make a basic ogantwa using a shelf or table or a cabinet. Each is dedicated to a certain Lwa.

To make this ogantwa work for your chosen Lwa, put an image of a saint or spirit. An example is St. Claire, who is a spirit capable of bringing about illumination and clarity. Other examples of images you can use are those of the Holy Virgin, Danbala (St. Patrick), Papa Legba, Papa Ogou (St. George, and Mater Dolorosa (Ezili Freda).

Just like water being important for an altar designed for general or multiple purposes, you also need a bowl or glass of fresh water placed on the ogantwa for it to work. As a devotee, you may need to put a bell or rattle there so you can easily call the spirits. Other items you should put in your shrine are a glass bowl designed for lamp making, olive oil, cotton wicks, white taper candles, and a small brazier you can use for the incense.

Baptize the ogantwa, too. This is the key to cleansing and blessing it before each use. Usually, you will be asked to burn frankincense then recite three prayers, like Our Father or Hail Mary, for a certain period. After that, sprinkle your ogantwa with holy water taken from Catholic churches. This should be enough to baptize the ogantwa. Once done, you can start using it to act as your focal point for meditation and prayer.

Chapter 6: How to Make a Gris-Gris Bag

A gris-gris bag is one of the most popular items used by Voodooists. It is extremely popular in the Voodoo community for many good reasons. The origin of this bag can be traced back to West Africa. It started due to the influences made by Muslim scholars, mystics, and healers. After that, the use of this bag got absorbed by the cultures in Africa. It contributed its shaping and transformation based on the local customs and beliefs in the country.

The original gris-gris contained a folded paper with a Quran inscription. You can see this inscription being written using special ink. You may also find significant numbers, symbols, and words on the piece of paper. It was tied and folded using a string then stored in a leather-made pouch. This way, one could easily put it on his body or affix it to a certain, meaningful location.

Let's dive deeper into what a gris-gris bag is and how to create one through this article.

Gris-Gris Bag Defined

A gris-gris bag refers to a powerful charm bag constructed from chamois or red flannel. Note that such a trait is unchangeable. This means that the bag's color, the chamois or red flannel, should remain fixed. If the gris-gris bag you intend to use makes calls for a certain color, put one piece of such material inside.

For example, if the bag needs an orange color, look for a fabric piece in that shade. Just cut a small piece from this material, then put it inside the bag. It should be enough to handle the required color correspondence. You can make this bag in a similar way you create a sachet or mojo bag. The only thing that distinguishes it from the others is that it needs to be a certain color.

In Voodoo, the gris-gris bag aims to offer protection from evil. Many Voodooists also believe that it is effective in bringing luck. Some West African countries also use it as a birth control technique. It comes in the form of a small bag made of cloth. Voodooists inscribe it with verses derived from their African ancestors. This inscription often comes with a ritual number of tiny objects. They then wear it on almost all occasions.

You can wear the gris-gris bag in any part of your body. It could be on your limbs, waist, or neck. However, remember that the exact spot where you will be wearing it is often linked to the bag's purpose. You may wear it for health, love, social harmony, or protection, and each specific purpose requires a different placement.

Ingredients for Your Gris-Gris Bag

The gris-gris bag will always play a major part in the Voodoo tradition. As a matter of fact, it is the predecessor of Voodoo dolls. You can still see the gris-gris bag being used today, particularly in the New Orleans tradition, to gain protection from evil, attracting love, and manifesting luck, career growth, and money.

This bag is around 5 x 8 cm and made from thin leather, suede, or flannel by tradition. It is also necessary to fill the bag with specific items and materials, including dried herbs, talismans, amulets, coins, bones, and crushed minerals. Every item or element placed in the bag has a specific symbolism and purpose.

Plants and Herbs

Plants and herbs are among the most commonly used fillers in Voodoo's gris-gris bags. Each has a distinctive symbolism and quality you have to consider during the preparation. Some examples are:

- Alfalfa – to attain luck in business and gambling. It is also perfect when planning to protect yourself from bankruptcy and other financial or money issues.

- Aloe Vera – to protect from negative forces and influences

- Anise – to attain spiritual protection from bad luck. It also boosts your physical abilities and brings luck and fortune.

- Bay leaf – to gain spiritual protection, success, and good health. You can also use it for your gris-gris bag to attain mental clarity, banish evil spirits, strengthen wisdom, and emerge as a victor over your enemies.

- Black pepper – to prevent unwanted visits

- Catnip – to attract love. Women can also use it to attract the male.

- Dandelion – to fulfill your desires
- Eucalyptus – to protect you from bad luck and get rid of unwanted and bad habits
- Licorice – to gain control or dominance over someone
- Parsley – to attract love and encourage fertility
- Rosemary – to dismiss evil spirits and promote the well-being of the entire family
- Sage – to attain purification, genuine happiness, and wisdom
- Sweet pepper – to gain luck, especially in business and when gambling. It also helps in removing stress.
- Thyme – to achieve tranquility and peace, get rid of nightmares, and preserve wealth
- Yarrow – to gain courage

Stones and Minerals

You can also fill your gris-gris bag with stones and minerals. For you to use them effectively, you have to crush them to dust first. After that, combine the crushed stones and minerals with dried herbs. You can use them for many things, including success, health, spiritual protection, and love. Here are a few of those that you can use:

- Agate – You can use the white agate if you want to attain good health and the dark-colored ones if you want to be lucky whenever you gamble.
- Amber – for luck and love
- Amethyst – for spiritual protection and better health
- Colorless quartz – for better health, peace, happiness, and protection

- Flint – for better health and protection against all forms of hazards
- Gold – to gain money, wealth, and success
- Jasper – to obtain protection from a wide range of negativities and unwanted results
- Moonstone – for protection against the dangers associated with love
- Topaz – for health and spiritual protection
- Turquoise – for health and protection against negative results

Other Materials and Objects

Besides the herbs, stones, and minerals, you can also fill up your gris-gris bag with various materials and objects holding various meanings. Among the most commonly used ones are:

- Nail – to gain protection from negative results
- Dollar sign illustration – to attain luck when gambling
- Keys – to attract love
- A piece of red brick – to attract success and money and gain household protection
- Magnet – to manifest fortune and attract gifts. You can also use it to get the attention of people.
- Ammonia – to promote cleansing and gain protection from harsh effects
- Sugar – to attract love and success in a romantic relationship. It is also meant to manifest money or profit into a business.
- Salt – to promote spiritual cleansing and get rid of bad luck

- Lodestones – It is advisable to use the lodestones in pairs to attract positive forces and repelling the negative ones.
- Cross – to represent your faith and attain blessing and spiritual protection
- Dice – to gain more luck whenever you take on a game of chance or gamble
- Coins – to attract prosperity and money
- Personal items, like hair, photos, or nail clippings – to connect the amulet's energy to a certain person
- A piece of feather or colored cloth – to increase the color correspondences of the amulet
- Written talisman on a parchment – to increase the planetary influences of the amulet or improve its intent even further
- A saint's card or medal – Add the suitable patron saint medal to further strengthen your intent. It is also helpful to invoke the saint or spirit's aid.
- Magical powder and oil – You may also add magical powders and oils to strengthen the amulet's intent.

The Actual Making of the Gris-Gris Bag

Making the gris-gris bag is not that complicated, provided you gather all the necessary things. You can use any of the special herbs, stones, and objects stated in this chapter to make it work. You may also want to fill it up with roots, personal effects, crystals, European sigils and seals, and other lucky charms. Aside from all those possible fillers, you can also add other colors into it based on magical symbolism.

To know how many items you should put in the bag, then the answer would be an odd number that is not less than three and not over thirteen. It is also crucial to bless the items while putting them inside the bag. Use holy water or anointing oil to dress up the entire bag, too.

After that, a smudge in any kind of incense. Speak some words of power to it, then breathe upon it. Those are effective rituals capable of activating the power of gris-gris. If you plan to practice New Orleans Voodoo, remember that the gris-gris bag they create is usually concealed from public view. You also have to prepare it ritually on an altar then consecrate it to the four classic elements – fire, air, water, and earth.

The actual creation of the gris-gris bag also requires you to remember a few points and rules, among which the following are worthy of note:

- Color symbolism will always play a significant role in creating the bag – Pick a color specifically designed for your needs.

- Fill the bag with items that can specifically meet your desired purpose.

- Dress up the bag with a kind of liquid. It could be holy water or anointing oil.

- Be extra cautious of the things you say when creating the bag. Remember that the words that come out of your mouth can create strong energy, becoming a major component of the gris-gris bag.

- Smudge or smoke with incense every ingredient you intend to put inside the bag – Do the same to the final bag, too.

- Place or sew into the bag a written petition – This petition needs to be written using a magical alphabet. Alternatively, you can draw a magical seal or sigil on parchment paper using magical ink. Place it inside or sew it into the bag. You may also want to add some magic squares and talismans to the bag.

- Speak powerful words when creating the bag – This is crucial in the activation of only divine energy.
- Give life to your gris-gris bag by breathing upon it.
- Respect and match each filler ingredient's symbolism to a certain gris-gris bag.
- Lubricate the bag's surface using an oil connected to your purpose.
- Use incense or candle smoke to fumigate the bag before each use.

Just remember those tips when making your own gris-gris bag. One final note to consider is to ensure that you already visualize your end goal. Determine what you genuinely intend to achieve from creating this bag. After that, constantly think about the manner through which it will come true.

Once you have completed your gris-gris bag, put it or hang it in an open and prominent place – one you can see easily while letting you concentrate on it in private. That way, it will always remind you of your wish. To use it in the right way, say your own heartfelt prayer. Just hold it in your palms with your two hands close together, then bring it up to your mouth. After that, activate the bag using your breath by blowing into it.

Another thing to remember is to recharge it. You can do so by soaking it in whiskey every Friday. To use it to prevent evil from getting inside your home, then hang the bag over your doorway. You may also want to use a leather cord so you can wear the bag around your neck.

Alternatively, you can take it with you anywhere by putting it in your pocket. Just put it at the right spot – the right pocket if you are a man and the left pocket if you are a woman.

Can You Make Gris-Gris Dolls?

Yes, you can make your own gris-gris doll. The only thing you have to do is to prepare a black fabric and make a doll from it. It should be small enough. Then fill the doll with symbolic things, like salt, saffron, powdered dog manure, crumpled newspaper taken from an obituary, gunpowder, and graveyard dirt.

Once you have this gris-gris doll, you can use it for your intended purpose. Note there are several ways for you to use and work with these Voodoo dolls that will be explained in the next chapter.

Chapter 7: Working With Dolls

Voodoo dolls tend to spark fear from anyone unfamiliar with what they truly are. Hearing about and seeing these dolls will most likely invoke bloodthirsty and violent scenarios, particularly those you have watched in films or read in books.

The most common belief about Voodoo dolls is that they are made by anyone who wants to gain revenge or has a grudge against their enemy. You will notice some pins that the one who made it uses to thrust into the doll. The maker will then curse his target with pain, death, or any other form of misfortune.

Now the question is, is this really what Voodoo dolls are all about?

What Are Voodoo Dolls?

A voodoo doll is a small human effigy constructed from a couple of sticks tied together to form a cross shape and create a body with both arms sticking out. You can then see this shape is covered by a triangular cloth in bright colors. There are also several cases when it uses Spanish moss to fill it out and maintain the form of the body. It has a head made of wood or black cloth.

This doll comes with rudimentary facial features, including a mouth, a pair of eyes, and a nose. Those who constantly make Voodoo dolls also decorate them using sequins and feathers. In most cases, there will be pins to insert into the doll for any intention or purpose.

The voodoo doll also comes in various forms – one of which is the gris-gris doll briefly mentioned in the previous chapter. You can also see the practice of using it in many magical traditions based on different cultures worldwide.

Generally, you can see this figure being used in Haiti's Vodou religion. It is used as a major part of the tradition brought over from Western Africa with tiny effigies called a *bocio* or fetish they incorporated to perform rituals. When the slaves from Africa were forced to move to the new world, the *caldoches* brought their tradition of using this doll with them.

African shamans used this doll to interact or communicate with the Lwa and their dead ancestors to gain guidance. Eventually, they noticed how reliable this tool was for that purpose. It is the reason you can still see this Voodoo doll being used for essential rituals.

The general use of this doll, though, is to heal. Contrary to what others believe, it does not primarily aim to cause harm to people. Some also use it to maintain an open line of communication to the world of the departed. This means they use it to contact their recently departed loved ones.

Eventually, though, using voodoo dolls became more expansive, especially after the mish-mash of Catholicism, Voodoo, Native American healing arts, and European folk magic. It prompted the use of this doll in various ways, like the one that involves colored pins.

Besides that, the voodoo doll is also said to promote love, protection, success, and healing, among many others. While the Voodoo religion is a mystery to some, it still carries tools designed to promote change, like the voodoo dolls.

Ideal Materials for Your Voodoo Doll

Are you interested in making your own Voodoo doll? Then take note there are several materials you can use for this purpose. Remember that you may create your desired doll based on how you want it. Just make sure that it will have a direct spiritual and materialistic connection to the one you intend to reach out to through it.

You can make your own Voodoo doll from any material you can get hold of – among which are:

- **Clay** – The voodoo dolls used in the Louisiana/New Orleans tradition were traditionally created from blue clay taken from the burrows of crayfish. It is also possible for you to use any kind of clay when creating yours.

  You just have to make sure that once you finish creating your Voodoo doll made of clay, you maintain the hollow void inside of it. This is the specific spot where you can put certain materials that belong to or symbolize your subject. One example is an herb. Once you have formed the doll, you can paint and apply to it any magical symbol.

- **Wax** – You can also use wax for your Voodoo doll project. Some consider this material as almost perfect in all aspects. One advantage of it is its flexibility. It also works great as it can retain its original form and shape. It means it is long-lasting.

Many of those who make Voodoo dolls prefer wax because they can easily portray the human form. It is also easy to carve magic symbols on this material. You can attach someone's hair to it, making it more effective in building a connection.

- **Spanish Moss** - This material is a classic for the New Orleans tradition. What is great about Spanish moss is that it works impressively as stuffing or fillers for furniture and pillows, among many other things. It is the main reason this material is famous in Southern US. You can also see many Louisiana sorcerers using it successfully. One version of the Voodoo doll made out of this plant is the traditional type with no legs.

- **Cloth** - You can also make your own Voodoo doll made of cloth. One example is a rag doll constructed out of a couple of strips of material. You have only to embroider them into two identical forms on both sides of the doll. This can leave a hole, which will let you fill the doll with magical items, like common moss and herbs.

- **Wood** - If you want a more primitive style, you can create your Voodoo doll from wood. Before using this material, one thing to remember is that it can only depict the form of humans with fewer details. The reason is that it can work as a portrayal in a more generalized manner.

Sometimes, you can carve the doll in just one wooden piece. You need to be extremely accurate and skillful when doing so. A simple version would be a thick tree branch that uses moss as a covering. You can then trim it with a cloth and carve a face to help the figure appear more realistic.

- **Paper** - It is also possible for you to create your own version of the Voodoo doll from paper. One way to use paper to create the voodoo doll is to turn the material into a pulp first. Soak the pulped paper and combine it with an adhesive component. After that, you can use the same methods as you would use with wax or clay.

Another way to do it is to apply paper layer by layer. Glue it to a similar composition, then form it into your desired doll. The good thing about paper is that you can easily use it as an alternative for other Voodoo doll materials, like clay and wax.

Besides the mentioned materials, you can also use modern ones, like foam, polyethylene, and plastic. You can use all the available materials you think you can transform into a doll.

Steps in Making Voodoo Dolls

Now that you know the materials you can use to create your own voodoo doll, it is time to familiarize yourself with the actual creation process. Here's how you can make one for whatever purpose or intention you have in mind:

Step 1 – Prepare the Materials

Make an authentic voodoo doll on your own by collecting all the materials you need first. Pick those materials that perfectly suit the purpose or intention you have in mind. You may use any of the materials mentioned earlier.

After that, stuff it with moss. In choosing the material for your doll, go for one to which you are strongly connected. In this case, allow your spirit to serve as your guide. Listen to what your spirit or Lwa is telling you, and you will be able to pick the right materials.

Apart from the materials you have to use for the doll's body, it is also advisable to gather items representing the subject or target of your spell. Remember that Voodoo practitioners strongly believe in sympathetic magic. This means that a human can transfer his energy to any inanimate object he touches or comes in contact with.

So, you can build a link between your target and the doll by collecting any of the target's personal items. These include clothes and hair - both of which are extremely powerful. Any object touched by the person works, too.

Step 2 - Form the Skeleton

You should then form the doll's skeleton. Note that your goal is to make it feel and look exactly the same as the one you intend to represent, particularly their basic anatomy. In that case, connect a couple of sticks using twine to form the t-shaped skeleton.

If possible, use natural materials for these as this can create an authentic doll. You can use pencils and pick a stick designated for the arms, head, and feet in the absence of branches or wood.

Step 3 - Stuff the Doll

This is similar to filling a stuffed animal. You have to wrap the formed skeleton using cotton, paper, shredded cloth, or feathers. If you want your Voodoo doll to become even more authentic, then use Spanish moss as stuffing. It is more natural, producing better and more authentic effects.

Step 4 - Pick the Material for the Skin

Your choice should depend on the actual spell you intend to use. Ensure that the material is large enough as you will be using it to cover the doll entirely. In most cases, this skin is based on fabric. You may also use an organic material or corn husk. Pick the appropriate color, too, as it can greatly influence the spell.

For instance, to cast a spell using the voodoo doll to manifest luck and wealth, choose green. You can also use natural fibers, such as muslin or hemp, to encourage fortune and luck.

Step 5 - Form the Head, Feet, and Torso

After wrapping your chosen fabric around the skeleton and stuffing, you can start making the head, feet, and torso. You can do so helped by a ribbon or twine. Once done, you can draw the face of the doll.

It should resemble the person who your spell targets, making the doll more effective. For instance, if that person has brown eyes, use brown buttons for the doll's eyes. Use brown yarn for the doll's hair if he has brown hair, too.

Step 6 - Decorate the Doll

Ensure that the added decorations are based on the specific purpose or intention you have in mind. These added ornaments and decorations can help make your Voodoo doll more powerful. One example would be a dollar bill or coin you should attach to the doll if your purpose is to use it for wealth. To attract love by casting a spell using the Voodoo doll, you can sew on or attach a heart to it.

Step 7 - Baptize It

The voodoo doll you have made also needs to be baptized. This will let you associate it with that name. It is also the key to turning it into the person you want your spell to target. Baptizing the doll is even more important if your goal is to hex someone. To baptize it, dunk it underwater while stating the verse for baptism.

It is also crucial to purify the doll. Some ways to purify the doll include dissolving sea salt in the water before the baptism, burning incense close to the doll's body so it can absorb it, and burying the doll underground to absorb the natural energy of Mother Nature.

Step 8 - Visualize

After you have finally created and baptized or purified your doll, you can start the visualization process. Just hold the Voodoo doll you have made, then visualize the end result. To use it to make someone fall for you, then visualize it. If you intend to use it to heal someone, it would be better if the ill person you want to cure is present during the visualization. That way, you can build a stronger connection between him and the doll.

How to Use the Voodoo Doll

Once you have finally created your Voodoo doll, you can use it for any purpose or intention you wish to come true. It could be love, guidance, empowerment, or healing. You can even use it for cursing, though it is still advisable to remind yourself not to use it to harm anyone. Some of these Voodoo dolls can also be used as talismans and teaching aids.

To be able to use the doll, incorporate the right colors to it. Remember that color has a great influence on the purpose you intend to attain. As a guide, here are the colors and what they can manifest.

- Red – love, power, and attraction
- White – healing, purification, and positivity
- Green – fertility, growth, money, and wealth
- Purple – psychic exploration, spirit realm, and wisdom
- Yellow – confidence and success
- Blue – peace and love
- Black – negativity. This means you can use it to dispel negative energy or for summoning it.

You can also find these colors on needles and pins you can stick into the Voodoo doll so you can make your intention come true. Usually, you can use it to address a specific person's spirit. It summons or calls upon a spirit through a Lwa, making them listen to your plea so you can manifest your wants, desires, and wishes.

To communicate or interact with a person's spirit, pin a personal token or charm to your doll. It could be a piece of clothing, a strand of hair, or a picture. It is possible to talk directly to his spirit through the doll. You may appeal to the spirit, persuade him to do something, or ask questions.

Another practical use of the voodoo doll is to serve as a focus tool designed for meditation, spells, and prayers. To make it work for that specific purpose, put it on your Voodoo altar or shrine so you can easily focus on it whenever you meditate, pray, or cast spells.

Add special items, such as anointing oils, so you can increase its power while also making your message a lot clearer. Another item you can add is candle magic, which works effectively to transmit your message clearly to the spiritual world.

There are several ways for you to use Voodoo dolls. One thing to remember, though, is that they are not completely evil. The majority of the rituals you can do while using the dolls are beneficial to your well-being.

However, several decades back, African slaves used these dolls to defend themselves secretly from their masters. The trauma brought on by that part of the community's history is probably why Voodoo dolls are mistakenly perceived as tools for causing vengeance and harm.

Yes, you can charge it any way you want, but ill-will, harm, and malice should never be part of your intentions. If you use it to cause harm to others, then you will likely gain karmic backlash in the end, like bad luck, conflict, and depression.

Traditionally, a priest or someone in medicine blesses it to carry healing light and positive vibrations and prevent it from being used to cause negativity. Also, try to do the same if you want to make the most out of your Voodoo doll.

Chapter 8: The Voodoo Way of Life

To be a Voodooist, you should make this religion a part of your life. You have to learn the Voodoo way of life to make it work wonders for you. There are daily routines and practices you have to follow if you want Voodoo to give you the results you want.

Remember that Voodoo requires you to act. You need to act on it as it is the only way to live and breathe the religion. Note that as a Voodoo practitioner, you need to be able to bring its principles to life. You can't just learn it passively. It requires you to participate in its practices actively.

For instance, each ritual and ceremony requires you to take action. You have to act and move. Among the things you have to do are salute, dance, play drums, sing, and draw or trace veves or Voodoo symbols. You will see no member of the community sitting while someone else preaches.

As a member of the Voodoo community, you also have to know that each day of the week will be dedicated to practicing Voodoo. Here's the daily routine that is so typical for most, if not all, Voodoo practitioners:

- **Sunday** – This is considered God's day. However, one thing to note is that Voodoo practitioners differ in terms of what they do on Sundays. Some commit not to perform any form of spiritual work. You will not see them saluting any Lwa and worshipping spirits and other objects.

They focus more on serving just one God as this specific day is so sacred to Him. To do the same, then you can dedicate Sundays as the perfect time to respect, remember, and worship God.

- **Monday** – Many consider this day as the start of the week. Monday is so sacred to the ancestors and Lwas, known as Legba and Gede. Since Monday serves as the week's opening, it is also the best time to take care of the same Lwa you have to care for before moving on to the next.

You can think of it this way. Right after worshipping and focusing on God on Sunday, which is His day, you have to take care of your ancestors. When that happens, you can expect everything to flow more easily, specifically working with the Lwa. It is here where you can expect Gede, along with his ancestors, to come in.

However, before you can call other spirits or Lwa, remember that you have to salute Legba, who serves as the gatekeeper, first. It is in Papa Legba's hands whether he will open up the doors for you or close them.

Once you have the first couple of days set up, you can expect the remaining days of the week to flow naturally. You just have to make sure that your rituals and routines focus on the Lwas or spirits, which are considered the most powerful on those days. Here is a guide:

- **Tuesday** – a sacred day to the spirits who are part of the Petro family. Knowing that, you have to focus your rituals on them, more particularly Ezili Danto.

- **Wednesday** – a sacred day for the Nago nation. Spirits or Lwas in this nation will be more powerful during this day. You can expect supreme power from Ezili Danto, more specifically.

- **Thursday** – This day is meant for the Rada family as the spirits here will likely bring out their superior power.

- **Friday** – This day belongs to Gede, more specifically Brijit and Baron.

- **Saturday** – It is the best day to have a grand ritual or ceremony as it is when all Lwas are powerful.

Serving the Lwas

One Voodoo routine and ritual you have to follow to ingrain this religion into your life is to serve a Lwa based on his sacred day. There are many ways to achieve such a goal – one of which is to wear the color of a particular Lwa on their day. Another routine you should strictly follow is to observe abstinence on that specific day. Voodoo rituals will also always involve serving them and singing with them throughout the ceremony.

Anyone married to a specific Lwa will have to observe and celebrate that Lwa's sacred day. Here, you can choose to wear specific clothes, prepare your bed in a specific manner, and do things capable of signifying the sacred commitment of the human spouse.

Worshipping Nature and the Ancestors

For understanding the way of life in the Voodoo community, getting to know more about worshipping nature and the ancestors is a must. Note that the primary belief of most Voodooists is there is only a single Creator, but such a supreme God is distant and can only interact through spirits. Because of that, spirits and spiritual communication are extremely popular in practicing Voodoo.

This belief is one reason why it is extremely important to worship ancestors and nature. As an animist religion, which consecrates a huge community to Lwas or spirits and ancestors, it is truly necessary to learn how to worship them. These ancestors constitute a system composed of religious rites and beliefs mainly used to reinforce the social system and family dependence. It also aims to reinforce voodoo spirits, deities, guardians, and forces of nature.

It is also crucial to worship ancestors as this can also help bring out the power of the spirits. Note that spirits are extremely powerful in the sense they can influence both nature and human existence. Every spirit is responsible for different facets or domains of life. Also, note that some of Voodoo's spirits are believed to be the souls of the departed.

However, it is necessary to worship them. It is a central belief regarding the power of spirits that combine ancestor worship and animism together, allowing the spirits of deceased loved ones, and the spirits of all-natural elements, to become powerful forces for someone to ask for help.

Daily Devotionals

Voodoo practitioners and devotees are famous for their ability to spend a huge portion of their life worshipping spirits or Lwas. Most offer blood sacrifices, prayers, and thanksgiving to the deities or spirits. They often perform such rituals to find advice, promote good fortune, and build a strong connection with the spiritual realm.

One of the most commonly used routines for Voodooists is to perform daily devotionals. It is a part of the daily life they commit to doing. A lot of Voodooists make it a habit to have a sort of daily devotional. This is especially true for Voodooists who serve the community to obtain their primary source of income. In this daily routine, it is crucial to set the goal of waking up the spirits or Lwas, so they can work with you. Doing daily devotionals the right way is also the key to opening your home and gaining clientele.

It is crucial to create your personal devotion to a specific Lwa every day. You just need to set aside a few minutes, even just five minutes or so, for this daily devotion. Note you may spend even just a short moment praying. You can make it either short or long. It also works well if you intend to get Lwa to work in your everyday life.

Besides the daily devotionals, you can also practice Voodoo through certain routines and rituals, including:

- **Possession, Which is a Sacred Ritual** – This specific ritual requires you to worship the possessed and then listen intently to what they have to say based on the messages of the spirit.

- **Taking Part in Ceremonies** - Ceremonies will always be part of the Voodoo community's routines. We call the Manje Yanm meant to celebrate the yam harvest with the first yam being offered to Lwa Ginen. Note that while this ceremony has no fixed date, you must do it whenever you harvest yam once you become part of the community.

- **Use of Voodoo Dolls** – Discussed in the previous chapter, the voodoo doll is a major part of the community. The goal of this doll is to symbolize or represent people whose energy you intend to influence or affect. As an example, you can create the Voodoo doll to attract someone into your life.

Just put the created doll in your bedroom so you can attract his energy. As a sacred object, you can also use the doll to release positive energy and promote healing and positivity, above many other things.

By practicing Voodoo, you can make positive changes in your life. All it takes is to practice it every day and serve a particular Lwa. As a way of life, this religion helps remove obstacles that may block your path toward success and happiness. Avoid using the Voodoo practice to hurt others, though.

To make it a part of your life, reflect on how exactly you can use it. You have to know how you can get the support and guidance of Lwas and deities. That way, you can also gain access to positive energy, making it possible for you to manifest only the good things in your life. Avoid being negative when casting your spells, for instance, as it may only cause you to encourage negativity instead of positive things.

Voodoo vs. Christian Traditions

As mentioned in previous chapters, Voodoo is a syncretized religion as it also has a link to Christian traditions. However, some things make the two distinctive, particularly in their traditions and rituals.

For instance, most Christians and Roman Catholics worship their God and saints in the church, cathedrals, chapels, basilicas, and personal dwellings. Voodoo devotees, on the other hand, worship their God and Lwas in temples and use altars. The two are the same, though, in the sense they need to worship higher beings and deities (the Lwas for Voodoo and saints for Christians, usually).

Voodoo and Christian practices also have similarities and differences. Christians, for instance, believe in praying and worshipping in church. They also practice reading the Bible and following the sacraments, communion, and acts of charity. Meanwhile, you can see Voodoo traditions focusing not only on prayer, daily devotion, and healing but also on witchcraft. Their traditions also include blessings, and they have clear distinctions between good and evil.

The main purpose of Christianity is to love God while obeying his commandments. The religion also puts more emphasis on spreading the Gospel to save others. In the Voodoo community, you can see their traditions and practices focusing more on honoring God and the Lwas. They also emphasize more on celebrating and honoring life. With that in mind, your daily life should focus more on healing and initiation if you intend to practice Voodoo.

Chapter 9: Invocation and Summoning Ritual

Among the most vital aspects of the Voodoo religion are invocation and summoning rituals. These rituals aim to call upon a specific Lwa based on the occasion being celebrated or the specific intention of the Voodoo practitioner doing the ritual. One of the most interesting things about Voodoo is the strong relationship between the dead and the living. It is life itself that also gives birth to Lwas and spirits that the followers have to summon, depending on their intentions.

Contrary to what other people believe, though, invoking or summoning spirits does not necessarily mean you must call upon the evil ones. It is even possible for you to invoke peaceful spirits, including deities, ancestors, and gods and goddesses. You can do that by chanting sincere prayers and peaceful responses.

Note that to invoke and summon a specific spirit or Lwa, music and chanting should always be present. The reason is that the spirits respond a lot better to dance rhythms, music, and chanting, is that doing this shows how the devotees worship, honor, and respect them.

Music and chants are necessary to address the spirit with respect, together with sincere prayers. With this included, there is a higher chance for you to succeed in bringing the spirit to life and allowing them to guide you throughout your everyday life and actions.

The act of summoning and invoking spirits can be considered as a highly advanced type of spell. The reason is that it requires you to call upon a higher being in the form of the spirit or Lwa and the deity. With that in mind, you should never take this entire process lightly. Avoid invoking an entity or spirit who does not want to be summoned lightly.

If you intend to summon a high-frequency spirit or entity, conduct all the necessary research about it first. Frequency, in this case, refers to the specific vibrational level through which an entity or spirit operates.

Importance of Purpose and Intention

Aside from music and chanting that serve as avenues to show respect to the Lwas, it is also necessary for you to have a distinct intention or purpose for summoning and invoking a Lwa. As a beginner, you have to know exactly your purpose or intention for summoning a spirit. There should be a distinct goal or purpose in mind. Knowing your exact purpose will be easier for you to strengthen your skills and focus on your attempt or the entire ritual.

Also, remember that the Lwa you are trying to summon will most likely listen if you can draw their attention to your presence. The invocation's actual purpose will also clearly show you the exact Lwa you should call upon. You can summon a specific spirit or Lwa for purposes like wealth, relationships, health, and social status. You can also invoke one to help you handle a certain problem.

Ensure that you have a good and valuable reason for summoning the spirit. Imagine them as grumpy people who do not want to be disturbed when asleep. With that said, your reason should be really good for calling upon them. You need not be in a life-or-death situation when doing so, but your purpose should be a good excuse to bother and wake them up. Only summon them when you require their help and assistance for a problem you can't solve independently.

How to Invoke or Summon the Right Lwa

To invoke the correct spirit or Lwa, you have to look for a summoning ritual specifically intended for them. You can learn some rituals and magic spells from books and other sources. You can also design and make your own. When choosing or creating rituals, remember that it often consists of three basics steps – building the most suitable atmosphere for the ritual, getting into the trance state, and summoning/invoking and interacting with the spirit.

Create the Perfect Atmosphere

Building the perfect atmosphere for your rituals should be one thing you have to do when invoking Lwas. If you are still new to this realm, you may wonder why rituals often look kind of sinister and scary. The reason behind this is that it builds up the right atmosphere that encourages the spirits to come out.

This first step aims to create a specific atmosphere in the area designated for the ritual. It is also crucial for the participants of the ritual to have the right mindset. You have to create a mindset of uniformity, self-sacrifice, and discipline and show it in the way you dress for the ritual and set up the designated place for it.

Now, the question is, what kind of atmosphere should you aim for when performing invocation and summoning rituals? The answer is an atmosphere capable of separating you from your mundane daily reality. You have to be in a different atmosphere – one that can convert your mind into a more spiritual state.

Getting Into the Trance State

The atmosphere you have created for the ritual should be the one that will bring you to the right trance state. Here, you will need to use the right sounds, objects, colors, and patterns to connect with your spiritual nature. Reaching the trance state, in this case, does not mean you must get rid of your sense of reality completely.

What you should be after is a theta brainwave state – one like you usually enter as you are falling asleep. It refers to the quiet area between being awake and experiencing your dreams. You have to penetrate this state as this is the most appropriate mental state for spell casting and conjuration.

For you to reach this state of mind, you can use one or a combination of these tools:

- **Veves/Sigils** - The veves or the Voodoo symbols we have discussed in one chapter of this book should be used to get into the trance state. Veves refer to the symbols of various spirits as previously discussed. Used for centuries, you can use them for your summoning rituals by looking directly at them.

    You can draw the veve yourself while the ritual is ongoing. Drawing it on your own is beneficial as it can give you a more trance-inducing experience, increasing your chances of getting into the desired trance state fast.

- **Enns** - These refer to sound frequencies that one can use when connecting with spirits and deities. You can chant these *enns* or use them as silent mantras. You may use them based on your discretion, provided the end result is the trance state.

- **Candles** - You also need to have candles around. This is crucial as you need to gaze at the flames of the candles to build a theta state. The reason is that it will let you focus your attention on the flame while also feeling relaxed. Another way to use the candles is to visualize the specific spirit you intend to invoke or summon. Just imagine this spirit manifesting in the flame, and you will have an easier time entering the trance state.

- **Some Pointy Objects** - Some examples are sword, dagger, and wand. They often serve as extensions of your hand. This is necessary as extending your hand will let you channel energy more effectively. It is like that scenario of you hitting someone using any of the mentioned objects.

However, the major difference is you do not use the objects for fighting or combat. What you do, instead, is charge a specific space or object by sending magical energy to it. You can charge a veve or sigil, magical circle, mirror, or anything that symbolizes the spirit you are summoning or invoking.

- **Magic Circle** - Sometimes, you may need to create a magic circle on the floor. You can mark a circle on the floor, which serves as the exact spot where you can trap the spirit you summon. You may also use this magical circle to protect where you stand or sit while you let the spirit linger or stay outside.

If you plan to use this element for your summoning rituals, remember that it usually requires you to make two circles. One should be for you, while the other should be for the spirit. The good thing about the circle is that it can create a form of separation.

It is great as the spirits may interfere with all the present energies in the area and people. Note, however, that using a magic circle is optional. A lot of those who regularly summon Lwas do not even use this element in their rituals.

- **Meditation** - You can also meditate to reach the trance state. One advantage of this technique is that you do not have to prepare ritual objects for it. The only things you need to reach the trance state through meditation are concentration and a clear mind. Meditate for around thirty minutes to cleanse your mind and get rid of all unnecessary thoughts, making it possible for you to reach the trance state quickly.

Using any or a combination of these tools and techniques, you can bring your mind into a trance-like state, making it possible for you to gain better results from the ritual. You may also use other items, like magic robes, gemstones, and crystal balls. The color of the items also matters a lot. For instance, you can use the color red to invoke warlike spirits. The goal is to use the elements with their corresponding elements and colors to create a trance-inducing state and an appropriate ritualistic atmosphere.

Invoking the Spirit

Now that you have prepared the perfect atmosphere for the ritual and reached the trance state, you can invoke the spirit or Lwa. The state you are in will make it easier for you to interact with spirits. This is mainly because your consciousness is already at that point where you can respond more effectively to such influences. Your goal is to invoke or summon the spirit in such a way it enters your body, allowing you to have its traits.

Avoid mistaking invocation for possession, though, as the two are different. If you are possessed, then it means that the spirit controls you. Invocation, on the other hand, leaves you in control. However, you will have many personality changes since you are already receiving the traits of your summoned spirit.

There, you should start calling for your chosen spirit. You can do it by saying formal incantations from various sources or writing your own rituals and using them. If you are gifted, then you can also rely on any form of inspiration that comes to you during the entire procedure.

It would be best for you to be more creative in your rituals as spirits prefer them. Ensure that you also make the entire ritual a unique and personal experience for you. Once you have successfully summoned the spirit, remember that you can command it. Avoid the mistake of humbling yourself too much. It would not be a great idea to act like a servant or slave when trying to communicate what you want.

Command the spirit as you are a conjurer. You are the creator or god of the entity you have summoned to this plane of reality. Avoid disrespecting the spirit, though. You can command it while still acting with respect, not only to the spirit but also to yourself.

Once you have successfully communicated your desire and got what you want, feel free to end the ritual. What you should do is to thank the spirit. Express how thankful you are for their presence, giving you answers to your questions, and providing guidance. Ensure that the candles you light up during the ritual continue burning until they go out on their own. After that, you can dispose of them. Avoid reusing the candles or any other items you have used for this ritual for another.

Basic Invocation Ritual

Now that you are aware of the usual steps for invoking spirits, here is a basic ritual you can follow.

Things You Need:

- Silver or white candle
- Gift for the spirit – You can offer anything as a gift, but you have to make sure that it fits and represents the spirit you wish to summon. Some great examples are drink, food, and tobacco.
- 1 cup of salt
- Sage smudge stick

Spirit Invocation Instructions:

1. Get rid of all the negative energies surrounding you. A wise tip is to prepare a cleansing bath. Just run lukewarm water in a tub, then add the salt to it. Soak your body in it for

20 minutes or so. After that, dry off, then wear something comfortable.

2. Cast a circle and ask for blessings.

3. Light the sage. Then smudge yourself as well as the area inside the circle. It is helpful to remove the negative energies still there. Allow the sage to continue burning after that.

4. Put the silver or white candle in a holder. After that, put your offerings or gifts around it.

5. Close your eyes, then breathe deeply. Your goal should be to focus more on being welcoming and open with your eyes closed and while taking deep breaths. Light the candle, then recite your prepared incantation or ritual.

6. Wait for the spirit to come to you. If you have successfully summoned the spirit, then ask your questions or request guidance or any other form of help you are seeking.

Invoking Papa Legba

Here is also an example of summoning a specific Lwa in the Voodoo community. In this case, it would be Papa Legba who you should invoke first as he is the gatekeeper of the spiritual world. It would be best if you knew exactly how you could summon Papa Legba, as he will be the one to open the gates for the spirits to come to you.

Here's what you will need for this invocation ritual:
- Red and black candle
- Rum
- Three coins
- Cigar
- Sugarcane juice

- Cookies and other sweets
- Groundnuts
- Veve of Papa Legba

Procedure:

1. Put everything on the altar, then light all the things that have to be lit, like the red and black candle and the cigar. Begin meditating.

2. If you feel ready, summon or call Papa Legba. One great thing about summoning Papa Legba is that language will never be an issue. Do not worry about whether Papa Legba understands you. Summon him by reciting or singing his prayer.

"Papa Legba, open the gate for me.

Antibon Legba, please open the gate.

Legba open the gate for me, and I will thank

the Lwa when I return."

3. Observe his response. If you feel like he is already around, you can ask for his help and guidance. Communicate with him, just like when talking to a friend. He will listen to whatever you want to say. Allow yourself to open up to him. After that, ask him respectfully to open up the gates so the other Lwas or spirits will come out. Be specific when mentioning the Lwa you intend to talk to.

4. After you send your request, offer him the items you have prepared on the altar. This should also be the perfect time to begin invoking the specific Lwa you wish to interact with. Remember, though, that each Lwa requires a different ritual. The reason is these spirits have different preferences.

5. Once you have successfully completed your invocation rituals to your desired Lwa, express your gratitude to Papa Legba. Thank him for listening to you and allowing you to

speak to a specific spirit. Then ask Papa Legba to close the gate as he returns to his world.

After completing the ritual, it would be best to gather all the offerings you have prepared. Bring them to a crossroad so you can drop off Papa Legba together with the gifts you offer him. Leave the offerings beneath a tree close to the crossroad or at the side.

Some Warnings to Keep in Mind

Regardless of what you are looking for, whether it's answers to questions, guidance, or help with any aspect of your life, you have to use the invocation ritual with caution. Do extensive research before you even start. Avoid rushing the process so you prevent mistakes that will lead to irreparable harm to you or anyone. Remember that while this activity is rewarding, it also has consequences if you do not do it correctly.

Chapter 10: Voodoo Cleansing and Protection Spells

The Voodoo spells you can cast may also promote cleansing. Remember that several waves and energies are surrounding you. Some of these energies are positive, while the others are negative. It is the reason you have to learn a few cleansing spells. You can cast them to bring more positive energies into your life and your household while getting rid of the negative.

Voodoo Cleansing Spells for Your Home

You may want to cast Voodoo cleansing spells if you feel like your home is already becoming full of negativity. Cleansing, in this case, refers to rituals you can perform to purify your space. It aims to eliminate stagnant, malicious, and negative energies and entities.

Several Voodoo practitioners perform cleansing rituals before casting spells because they fear any negative presence. They also do it solely for their home's general upkeep. You can cleanse all spaces and objects in your home. The people inside your home can even be cleansed. Usually, you will need to use cleansing tools that are personal for you for the spells and rituals to become even more effective.

There could be various reasons for you to cleanse your home. It could be either positive or negative. One reason is that you may just have moved to your home and wish to celebrate your new space by anointing, blessing, and purifying it.

Another potential reason is the presence of negative energy in your house which you want to eliminate or clear. Negative energy can be linked to spirits. It could be that someone died in the house naturally, by choice (suicide), or through a murder. Note, however, those are not the only reasons for negative energy to come out. Human behaviors may also trigger it.

For instance, if something negative happens inside the home due to the behavior of someone living there, you can't clean this negative energy unless he completely stops the negative behavior. With that said, you have to discover first if anyone in your household contributes to the piling up of negative energy before casting Voodoo home cleansing spells.

Among the scenarios that may require you to do the Voodoo cleansing for your home would be:

- Living in a house that has a violent and disturbing history
- Traumatic events that happened inside the household
- Recent burglary
- Spooky feelings and vibes inside the house
- Constant arguments with partner or family members with no viable reason
- Restless sleep
- Crying with no reason
- Sudden illnesses

- Desire to manifest luck, love life, good relationships, and a new job or house
- Desire to improve an area or aspect of your life

If you have experienced any of the mentioned scenarios, you may want to consider casting Voodoo cleansing spells and rituals. Before that, though, remember these tips:

- **Clean Your House Thoroughly** - Remove all junk from your homes as well as anything inside it that is depressing. Clean all parts of your home, including the garage, attic, and basement. After that, gather a lot of things you find pleasing and let them surround you. It could be pictures of your loved ones, attractive flowers, and your favorite ornaments. Surround yourself with uplifting and pleasing things so you can begin inviting positive energy.

- **Allow Sunlight, Fresh Air, and Other Forms of Nature to Penetrate** - Allow your home to receive natural light or sunlight for a few days before the ritual or spell. This is necessary to let fresh air get in, too, which is a huge help when moving energy. The sunlight will always have a cleansing and revitalizing effect. If possible, put some living plants around your home. Their nature is known for emitting energy healing traits.

- **Open All Doors** - Ensure you also open every door in your home. It could be your house's main door or your French windows, closet, drawer, cabinet, oven, and microwave, among many others. It is the key to removing negative and dark energy and taking them out from hiding.

- **Walk Counterclockwise** - Before doing your house cleansing rituals and spells, make sure that you are walking counterclockwise - walking to the right while being close to the walls all the time. It is necessary as this direction can help to banish and drive out all negative energies. After clearing a specific room, ensure that you use the same door you used to enter to exit if that space has at least two doors.

Using Candles for Cleansing

To get rid of negative energy from your home and any earth-bound souls staying there, white candles combined with house cleansing prayers can help. White symbolizes enlightenment, and the candles in this color can draw such a form of enlightenment from the light. A blessed herbal candle containing sage, cypress, and lemongrass blend may also be used as an alternative.

To use the candle, set your intention of removing negative energy and dark entities from your home. Light the candle, then say your chosen house cleansing prayer. This prayer could be something like, "Dear Supreme God, remove all negative energies from this home. Bless and cover it with your pure and genuine white light of protection and love."

Repeat this prayer several times to affirm your desire and intention. You can expect the light from the candle to respond to you and guide you.

Using Sea Salt for Cleansing

Sea salt is also another effective tool for cleansing your home. It allows you to remove all forms of disturbance and dark energy from your home safely and effectively. The good thing about sea salt is that it has a strong cleaning power, which significantly improves its cleansing ability. You can use it for your home and office cleansing rituals. Here's how.

1. Clear your mind from all thoughts. Set an intention to remove negative energy from your home.

2. Spread the sea salt on your home's exteriors. Spread it on every window, step, and doorway. When doing this, say this spell loudly:

"Remove all negative energies and entities from this place. Only those who love purely may enter this home".

3. Repeat it until you have spread the salt completely around your house.

4. Put some sea salt into small bowls. If possible, fill each bowl, then put one in every room in your house. Let it stay there for at least 24 hours so it can absorb all dark and negative entities.

5. Once the 24-hour period is up, throw the sea salt away. Make sure that the used salt is no longer part of your house.

Using Incense for Cleansing

It is also possible for you to take advantage of incense's vibrational frequency to help remove house-bound spirits and dark entities. Using incense in cleansing and clearing your home will allow you to deal with a certain vibration and universal force, which can naturally enhance the vibes within your home.

Sandalwood is an example of incense you can use for house cleaning. It works to awaken your chi or life force. Other great choices are sage and lavender. To cleanse using your choice of incense, do the following:

1. Open all windows, doors, drawers, closets, and any other item in your home with doors like the oven and microwave.

2. Build your strong intention of clearing your place before the actual home cleansing.

3. Once you already have your intention, you can burn a stick of incense. Put it in the specific room in your house you think requires thorough cleansing.

4. Walk counterclockwise. You can do that by keeping close to the walls and the right side when walking.

5. Wave the lighted incense beneath your furniture, bedding, and around the walls of your closets. Say the prayer or mantra to remove all negative energies and unwanted vibrations from your home.

How to Cleanse Your Body

Note that your body may also be filled with many negative energies, spirits, and vibrations, just like your home. Fortunately, you can also cleanse it helped by Voodoo spells. Here are a couple of ways to do so:

Cleansing Bath Spell

For this spell to work, you need a white candle and seven dried dandelion flowers. You can cast this spell through these steps:

1. Prepare yourself to take a warm bath.

2. Get the dried dandelion flowers, then crumble them in the water. Recite this spell seven times as you drop each flower:

"Bare vindeca bare!"

3. Get the candle and light it up. Allow yourself to get completely immersed in the water. Then say the following spell seven times:

"By virtue of the Supreme God and the Lwas. Bare and Vindeca.

Purify my body. Bare and Vindeca.

Purge my soul. Set it free from evil. Protect it from evil spirits. So be it."

4. Use the water to snuff the candle.

5. Spend a few minutes meditating. Visualize your body. Imagine it glowing with light. After that, you can complete the ritual by getting yourself out of the water.

Cleansing Water Spell

One advantage of this spell is that it is something that you can do quickly. It works for beginners, too. Among the things you need for this spell are one glass of water, coarse salt, and three white candles. To do it, here are the steps:

1. Form a triangle from coarse salt. Put the glass with water inside the triangle.

2. Place each candle in the triangle's vertices. Light them all.

3. Recite the following ritual afterward:

"Supreme God, Father of the Universe, purifies this water.

May it be purified in your name

Purify this liquid, make it blood, make it holy.

How sacred is the blood of your Divine Son, as your word is sacrosanct.

Word of love and justice. Forever and ever. So be it!"

4. Drink the water and allow all the candles to burn out.

Voodoo Spell of Protection

Besides being useful for the body and home cleansing, you can also cast Voodoo spells for protection. It is great, especially if you know exactly how you can protect yourself if another practitioner hexes you. A hex refers to a curse or magical attack, which may be intended to cause you harm. Note that despite the constant reminder that Voodoo should not be used to harm someone, there are still a few practitioners who do it.

There are two forms of curse or magical attack that may be used against you. It could be a direct curse or hex, operated against you helped by the suitable cursed material. This can be of a distinct nature, like herbs, menstrual blood, or powdered bones of anyone who has died. It can represent a sensitive instrument that allows evil to exercise power.

The cursed material is then sent to you in a few ways – adding it to your drinks or foods or being in contact with an object close to it. One example is your braided hair combined with blood and other kinds of materials placed within a mattress or cushion.

There is also what we call an indirect curse, which occurs via transference. This means resorting to certain things and objects representing you. It could be your clothes, puppets, or pictures.

How to Break a Curse or Hex

You can also break or purge a curse or hex and cleanse yourself, which is a good thing, especially if you never want to harm yourself. One way to do so is to use an amulet. Usually, this involves taking objects properly spellbound, personalized, and prepared with you all the time. It helps to ward off evil desires and vibrations. You can expect such elements to weaken the spell's effects, preventing it from hurting you.

Some of the amulets you can use for protection are crystals, a cross, or a pentagram. You can put an amulet or two inside your pocket or wear one around your neck. Other ways to break a curse or hex are:

- **Use Magic Herbs and Salt Baths** – You can use these items to cleanse and ward off the intentions of evil, particularly from those that intend to destroy you. Perform this ritual by preparing the appropriate atmosphere. You can do so by lighting a few candles then letting your bathtub filled with warm water.

Attract good fortune by thinking of pleasant and positive thoughts when doing this routine. You can make its healing power even stronger by adding or spraying it with salt, basil, absinthe, patchouli, and hyssop.

• **Burn Salt** - You can also remove a curse by burning salt. It cleanses and purifies, allowing another cycle of life to start. It also helps maintain the beauty of life. Spiritually, this technique can purify and neutralize psychic and negative energies in different cultures.

To protect yourself from curses and hex, or avoid them as much as possible, know how to burn salt correctly. The first thing to do is light up a fire-based wherever spot is convenient for you. It could be in your fireplace or burning charcoals spread on the ground.

Get some coarse salt, around a handful of it. Think of each negativity you wish to remove. After that, rub the salt on your skin for purification. After that, throw the rubbed salt into the embers or fire. To be honest, this technique can either produce fast and dry results or progressive and slow ones. Do which one you feel is ideal for you.

The fire from the candle works to burn the salt. It causes the salt to burst then raises the flame. By completing this ritual, you can finally set yourself free from all negative energies and the hex or curse being cast on you.

• **Burn Incense** - You may also want to burn incense to break a hex or curse. The good thing about incense is that it has a genuine cleansing effect. It breaks the spell or curse then throws out bad energy. It would be much better for you to use the incense and other herbs to significantly enhance its power.

To take advantage of it, but the incense together with the herbs you intend to use. Use a thread to tie them together. With that, you can expect them to be burned thoroughly and much faster. After consuming everything through the fire, you will notice its positive effects. Also, it helps to get a few branches of plants like sage and put them between the layers of your clothes. Doing so can help to ward off evil spirits.

Before taking advantage of any of the techniques mentioned for your next ritual, it also helps to remind yourself of:

- Avoid eating red meat.
- Avoid drinking coffee for a couple of weeks before the ritual and two more weeks after that.
- Smoking and alcohol are not allowed.
- Attend rituals and ceremonies in temples.

You can do several things to protect yourself from danger, especially from those who intend to harm you through magical attack, curse, or hex.

Chapter 11: Voodoo Love Spells

Voodoo magic is also so impressive that it can help you attain happiness regardless of where you are. There are Voodoo love spells that you can use to find love. One great thing about these Voodoo spells is that they are effective, plus they work fast. These spells are so swift that right after you cast them on your desired target, you can expect your intention to travel directly to their conscience.

With that, your target will surely develop a different idea, perception, and thought about you right away. Also, Voodoo's love spells can be used for a wide range of love-related motives we will discuss in this chapter.

Voodoo Spell to Make Someone Fall in Love

You will be using a Voodoo doll for this spell. This doll will represent the specific person you are targeting. By casting the spell, you can change how your target looks at you. The spell even aims to make your target fall in love with you. Here are the things you need for this spell:

- Voodoo doll representing your desired partner
- A personal item from your desired partner
- Something personal that you own
- White paper
- 3 ribbons – 1 each in the colors black, white, and red
- White candle
- Red ink with a feather serving as a pen

Create the Voodoo doll on your own using materials like clay, wax, or a piece of fabric you sew by hand. Put something used by your intended partner into the doll. It could be their hair or nail clipping. You also have to integrate something from you into the doll. Carve the name of your subject into the doll. Once you have prepared the Voodoo doll, you can start casting this spell.

Instructions:

1. Do this love spell on the day after the New Moon. This often happens on a Friday.

2. Prepare your Voodoo altar. You can do so by using a wooden match to light up the candle.

3. Get the three ribbons, then use them to wrap or cover the Voodoo doll. Ensure that you knot the ribbons together. While wrapping and knotting the doll with the ribbons, make sure to say the following aloud:

"These tapes tie you up

and weave your heart to mine."

4. Get the red ink and paper. Use it to write your target's name. Place the paper with the written name on your altar.

5. Put the Voodoo doll on a sheet, then blow out the candle.

6. Light the candle again the following night.

7. Take the Voodoo doll, then put it closer to the flame. You should then say,

"For you, I crave

for me, you burn."

8. Let the Voodoo doll rest on the prepared sheet. Do not blow out the candle. Let it continue burning for one hour or so.

9. Wrap your Voodoo doll using an object in red, then store it in a place that makes it safe.

Voodoo Spell to Bring Back Your Ex

If you still love your ex and you truly want to get back together with them, then know there is also a Voodoo spell you can use for that. For this specific love spell, you will need:

- Two voodoo dolls made by you - one is representing you while the other representing your ex.
- White candle
- Red candle
- Some offerings, like fruit and chocolates
- Red string

Instructions:

1. Light the white candle before doing the love spell.

2. Let your mind relax, then do not let your eyes look directly at the flame.

3. Think about your happy moments together and reminisce. Doing this is important as it helps build a positive vibe capable of getting rid of bad energy that can positively influence your love life.

4. Light the red candle, then put it beside the white candle.

5. Prepare the necessary offerings. They could be chocolates, fruit, or perfume. Put these offerings on a plate.

6. Create a couple of dolls, too. They should symbolize you and your ex. Then allow the two dolls to sit at the table. Ensure that they are facing each other.

7. Say your prayer or cast your spell, just like the one in the previous chapter. The spell or prayer's intent should be to bring your ex back to you and make your relationship and connection stronger this time.

8. Tie the dolls together using a red string. Make sure that the faces of the dolls touch each other. After that, hide the dolls in a secure place. Blow out the candles once done.

Voodoo Break-Up Spell

If you are no longer happy with your romantic partner, but you have a hard time breaking up with them, then there is a voodoo spell that can help you. You can also use this spell to make a couple of break up. Some things you need for this purpose are:

- Black candle
- 7 nails
- Recent pictures of the couple you wish to break up – If it is your romance you want to break, then prepare your own picture and that of your partner.
- 2 tbsps. cayenne powder
- 1 tbsp. garlic powder
- 2 tbsps. mustard seeds
- 1 cup
- Vinegar

- Salt
- A small bowl
- A string
- A sheet of paper

Instructions:

1. Use vinegar to anoint the black candle.

2. Get the nails and use them to poke the black candle. This can divide the candle into seven even or equal parts. The seventh pin or nail should be down at the bottom.

3. Mix the salt, mustard seeds, cayenne pepper, and garlic powder in a small bowl.

4. Place the paper in front of the black candle you prepared. Light it up.

5. Put the pictures over the sheet of paper.

6. Call upon a spirit and ask for help. Be forthright and honest when petitioning a spirit and seeking his help.

7. Get the lighted candle, then let the candle drip up to 9 drops of wax onto each picture. Sprinkle the mixture on top. Allow the candle to burn until it gets to the first nail. Snuff it out.

8. Take the first pin out of the candle the following day. Place this pin over the pictures. After that, light the black candle again. Do the same steps when it is time to take the candle, then drip the same number of wax drops onto the pictures. However, remember this time, let the candle burn to the next nail - after which, you have to snuff it out again.

9. Do the same on the remaining pins or nails. Repeat the steps for seven days. The 7th day should serve as the final ritual. Here, you will have to wrap the contents together with the pictures by tying them securely with paper.

10. Once done, you can also burn the doll and its contents while the ritual is still ongoing. You can then bury the ashes next to a tree or burn the doll in a cauldron. In this case, you must throw the ashes into the wind.

Attract Love With a Gris-Gris Bag

You can also attract new love through a Voodoo spell that involves the use of a gris-gris bag. Know this bag is extremely powerful for drawing out a new love. It would be best for this gris-gris bag to be constructed out of red fabric because aside from being powerful, it also works effectively for casting spells designed to attract love.

For this purpose, you need to gather all the items you have to put inside the bag to make the love spell work. These include:

• Something designed to help the energy connect to you - This could be a nail, body fluid, or hair.

• Herbs linked to attracting new love - Among the herbs you can use for this purpose are lavender, cinnamon, patchouli, catnip, basil, vanilla beans, daisy, valerian, and chili pepper.

• Stones capable of drawing love, like ruby, pearl, emerald, rose quartz, and rough diamonds.

Instructions:

1. Set the casting of the love spell at the appropriate time and day. The best time to do it is usually on a Friday night. It should be on the moon's waxing phase, preferably Venus' planetary hour.

2. Put everything you wish to use in the bag inside a bowl. Ensure that you choose those that are truly powerful in attracting love.

3. Place your right hand on top of the bowl. Your goal is to let the energy flow into the items inside.

4. Picture vividly the kind of love you wish to attract and accomplish using the gris-gris bag. This should take around 20 minutes. Your goal is to let your mind clearly see the end result as it can motivate you.

5. Put several drops of magnet oil into the bag every Friday. Once you feel comfortable with how it manifests your desire, you can bury it in the earth.

A Warning When Casting Voodoo Love Spells

One thing to remember for casting love spells is that you should avoid using them to harm someone. Note that voodoo attraction love spells require physical transmission by using items and objects that belong to the person subjected to the spell.

Despite being unique, the spell's final results should adhere to all the love spell principles. Some rules and principles you have to follow include:

- Not harming anyone
- Not causing negative side effects for the long term
- Not deceiving the subject

Also, it is necessary to make sure that the strongest spirit present when casting the love spell is that of the ancestors. Their power should be enough to remove all obstacles associated with love. Remember that while Voodoo spells are mainly designed to attract love, others also aim to rekindle the flame.

Another thing to remember is that casting Voodoo spells will always have risks. For instance, if you cast a love spell on someone, remember that it will cause your soul to become bound to them forever. With that said, avoid using a love spell on someone who you just lust after without the intention of being with them forever.

Most of these love spells will bind you. It would be like making an oath to the spirits or ethereal energy patterns you are serious about producing powerful love energy – one that the entire universe can take advantage of only if the spirits you summon change the material plane's energy in your favor. Your goal, therefore, is to make the results lasting, especially if you are after attracting the love of your life.

Overall, your goal should be to produce effects that will harm no one. Remember that if you use spells that harbor bad intentions, then it will likely turn into a self-curse, *so be extra careful.*

Chapter 12: Ceremonies and Festivals

As a form of belief system and religion, Voodoo also has its own ceremonies and festivals. They have their own holidays and religious celebrations. Some of these events are their unique spin on the holidays and events honored by other religions, especially Christianity and Roman Catholicism. The fact that Voodoo has already become an official religion since 2003 gives the priests in this community the right and authority to hold baptismal and wedding ceremonies, too.

When trying to learn about the popular ceremonies and festivals, note that it encompasses various aspects derived from Haiti's original inhabitants and the African freed slaves, Voodoo folklore, and Roman Catholicism. The following are just a few of the many ceremonies, festivals, and celebrations enjoyed by the Voodoo community.

Mange Loa

Mango Loa refers to a Voodoo ceremony, which involves a huge feast of all Lwas. This means it involves feeding the Lwas or deities and spirits. Any Voodoo ceremony that requires animal sacrifices and offerings is considered as a Mange Loa. During this ceremony, a lot of offerings will be served to the Lwas.

Aside from animal offerings, like chickens, bulls, and birds, the community will also offer cakes, syrups, and drinks to the Lwa. This celebration often takes place during the 2nd to 3rd week of January every year. Devotees and followers of the Voodoo religion strongly believe that the powers of Lwas increase significantly when celebrating this event.

Ouidah Voodoo Festival

Happening every 10th of January, the annual Ouidah Voodoo festival is a national celebration in Benin, honoring the traditional religion and its cults. It is even considered the largest gathering of all Voodoo devotees and practitioners in the world. It has the same level of importance as the celebration of Christmas to Christians.

Fortunately, you can attend this event even if you are not a full-blown Voodoo practitioner. You can just enjoy and observe how they celebrate this event. Certain aspects of this festival are not suitable for those with a faint heart, but it is a great way for you to become more enlightened about this misunderstood religion.

During this celebration, expect to see the ritualistic animal sacrifices made by practitioners. Another unique and controversial act during this event that may not be for the weak and squeamish is a sacrifice involving a priest ripping the chicken's neck using his teeth.

This event will also open up some markets full of wood carvings, masks, and fetishes. You will also notice women dressing themselves up with vivid rainbow colors. You may want to participate in this celebration, especially to grab the chance to witness the region's traditional and unique yet controversial culture.

Fat Gede

Also called the Day of the Dead, the Fat Gede is an annual national holiday in Haiti, the counterpart of All Saints' and All Souls' Day in the Roman Catholic religion. This event is celebrated on November 1 and 2, similar to the dates used in the Catholic religion. This is the time when Voodoo followers honor their dead ancestors.

Just like Catholics, Voodoo practitioners also tend to visit cemeteries to pray. They also light candles and offer flowers, drinks, and food to their departed loved ones. One thing that makes it distinctive from the celebration of Catholics is that Voodooists tend to continue the event in their Voodoo temples called peristyles. They celebrate this day with dancing and rituals for the whole night.

Bath of Christmas

Another great example of syncretizing Catholic celebrations with Voodoo is the Bath of Christmas, also celebrated by Voodoo devotees and practitioners every December 25. Some Voodoo houses celebrate Christmas Eve (Dec. 24), while other places do it for three days – from December 24 to 26.

This celebration involves Voodoo practitioners rubbing themselves using medical creams. They also rub talismans on their body to attain fortune, luck, and protection. The entire celebration also involves sacrificing animals, like pigs, turkeys, and goats, to honor a Lwa.

One great thing about Christmas Baths for Voodoo is that they are naturally cleansing. They also recognize how powerful these baths are as they can remove all negativity, restraints, curses, and evil spirits lurking around you.

During this event, you must summon and call upon the spirits to integrate their energy into the bath. Aside from sacrifices and offerings, it also involves singing and dancing to heat up the Christmas bath. This makes it more effective in washing out all the things that bind and restrict you, including doubts, aggression, anger, and limitations. This results in you becoming a more renewed person with a lot of potential.

Voodoo Fest

Another famous celebration that is part of the Voodoo tradition is the Voodoo Fest, which happens every October 31. In most cases, the celebration is a multi-day art and music festival that everyone can participate in for free. This annual festival celebrates Voodoo's several significant contributions to the culture and traditions in New Orleans.

It primarily aims to honor the ancestors and Lwas. It also intends to educate everyone regarding this religion while preserving and celebrating the distinctive cultural and spiritual New Orleans heritage. The Voodoo Fest is a fun and exciting celebration with plenty of interesting activities, including music and arts.

This event also exhibits several educational and cultural presentations, doll making and drumming workshops, and consultations with the leading practitioners of Voodoo in the city. You can expect this to be a fun and exciting day with rituals for ancestral healing.

Gran Bois

Another Voodoo holiday with a mark in the community is the Gran Bois. This holiday pays tribute to Grand Bois, its namesake that means great wood. It is nature's elemental power with a strong relationship to herbs, medicinal plants, and trees. Grand Bois is also considered the counterpart of St. Sebastian in the Catholic religion, who was venerated as the protector of illnesses. The holiday dedicated to Grand Bois will involve many offerings, including herbs, spiced rum, and honey.

A Voodoo Calendar

Besides the famous festivals, holidays, and events that honor the Voodoo religion mentioned in this chapter, here are other activities and events that all Voodoo practitioners and devotees observe every year:

January 17	Feast of Ogun (Yoruba)
February 1	Feast of Mama Brigitte
February 1	Feast of Oya
March 17	Feast of Damballah
March 20	Feast of Legba Zaou
March 24	Day of Blood
March 25	Feast of Oshun
April 23	Feast of Ogun (Santeria)
May 25	Feast of Ochossi
June 16	Death Anniversary of Marie Laveau
June 21	Feast of Babalu Aye
July 2	Feast of Expectant Mothers

July 16	Feast of Ezili Danto
August 25	Feast of Agasou
September 8	Feast of Oshun
September 10	Marie Laveau's birthday
September 24	Feast of Obatala
September 29	Feast of Eleggua
September 30	Feast of Shango
October 4	Feast of Orunmila
October 24	Feast of Erinle
November 1-2	Feast of the Dead
Full moon in November	Feast Day of Baba Yaga
November 25	Feast of Oya
December 4	Feast of Shango
December 10	Feast of Ganga-Bois
December 17	Feast of Babalu Aye
December 31	Feast of Yemaya

The Voodoo community has a lot of celebrations and events in store for its followers. These festivals and celebrations are among the ones they look forward to every year as those also allow them to show how they worship their deities, Lwas, and their Supreme God, Bondye.

Conclusion

The Voodoo religion is a mystery for many, riddled with many secrets coupled with many spells, rituals, beliefs, traditions, and ceremonies that others may misunderstand. It does not have a world authority or a scripture. It centers more on community and supports each individual's experience, and responsibility, and empowerment.

Because of that, it is not surprising to hear and see many misconceptions about it, along with negative depictions. Fortunately, you have been given a chance to change that through this book, which aims to open your eyes to what Voodoo truly is. I hope it has helped you understand everything about Voodoo and understand how it embraces and covers every aspect of the human experience. With that, it is truly one of the most meaningful and valuable religions ever introduced to the world.

Here's another book by Mari Silva that you might like

SANTERÍA

THE ULTIMATE GUIDE TO LUCIMÍ SPELLS, RITUALS, ORISHAS, AND PRACTICES, ALONG WITH THE HISTORY OF HOW YORUBA LIVED ON IN AMERICA

Your Free Gift (only available for a limited time)

Thanks for getting this book! If you want to learn more about various spirituality topics, then join Mari Silva's community and get a free guided meditation MP3 for awakening your third eye. This guided meditation mp3 is designed to open and strengthen ones third eye so you can experience a higher state of consciousness. Simply visit the link below the image to get started.

https://spiritualityspot.com/meditation

References

Admin. "Voodoo Magic Spells.Psychics Articles and History about Voodoo." Voodoo Magic Spells.Psychics Articles and History about Voodoo, 14 Jan. 2012, magicvoodoospells.blogspot.com/2012/01/how-to-make-gris-gris.html.

Alvarado, Denise. "The Voodoo Hoodoo Spellbook: How to Make a Gris Gris Bag." The Voodoo Hoodoo Spellbook, 20 Dec. 2012, voodoohoodoospellbook.blogspot.com/2012/12/how-to-make-gris-gris-bag.html.

Alvarado, Denise M. "Ritual Symbols of the Voudou Spirits: Voudou Veves." Exemplore, Exemplore, 8 July 2008, exemplore.com/magic/voodooveves.

Beautiful, Tragic. "Simple Cleansing Spells." Tragic Beautiful, https://www.tragicbeautiful.com/blogs/style-blog/simple-cleansing-spells.

Coles, Donyae. "Creating Your Altar: A Beginner's Guide." Spiral Nature Magazine, 15 May 2017, www.spiralnature.com/spirituality/altar-beginners-guide/.

"Creating Shrines and Altars for Healing from Grief." GoodTherapy.org Therapy Blog, 31 Aug. 2011, www.goodtherapy.org/blog/shrine-altar-grief-healing/.

DHWTY. "The Origins of Voodoo, a Misunderstood Religion." Www.ancient-Origins.net, www.ancient-origins.net/history-ancient-traditions/origins-voodoo-002933.

"Everything about the Art of Witchcraft - Magickal Spot." Magickalspot.com, magickalspot.com/.

Guilberly Louissaint. "What Is Haitian Voodoo?" The Conversation, 21 Aug. 2019, theconversation.com/what-is-haitian-voodoo-119621.

"Haiti: Introduction to Voodoo." Faculty.webster.edu, faculty.webster.edu/corbetre/haiti/voodoo/overview.htm.

"HAITIAN VODOU, VODOU RELIGION, VOODOO & VODOUN." Haitian Vodou, Voodoo, Las 21 Divisiones and Sanse, ezilikonnen.com.

"Haitian Voodoo." Traveling Haiti, 13 Jan. 2016, www.travelinghaiti.com/haitian-voodoo/.

HoodooWitch – Experiential Hoodoo Education for Everyone. www.hoodoowitch.net/.

"How to Build an Ancestor Altar." Crescent City Conjure, crescentcityconjure.us/blogs/city-of-conjure/how-to-build-an-ancestor-altar.

"How to Do a House Blessing Spell for Protection & Cleansing." Project Fey, https://www.projectfey.com/blogs/magical-musings/6062912-how-to-do-a-house-blessing-spell-for-protection-cleansing.

https://www.facebook.com/learn.religion. "Guide to the Beliefs and Religions of the World." Learn Religions, 2018, www.learnreligions.com/.

https://www.howstuffworks.com/tracy-v-wilson-author.htm. "How Voodoo Works." HowStuffWorks, 16 Feb. 2007, people.howstuffworks.com/voodoo.htm.

"Introduction to Voodoo - What Is Voodoo?" Wishbonix, 18 Feb. 2020, www.wishbonix.com/voodoo/

July 2015, Peter Moore | 17. "4 Intense Voodoo Festivals around the World." Wanderlust, www.wanderlust.co.uk/content/4-intense-voodoo-festivals-around-the-world/.

Kennon, Alexandra. "A Conversation with a High Priest of Vodou." Country Roads Magazine, 25 Sept. 2020, countryroadsmagazine.com/art-and-culture/people-places/the-truth-about-louisiana-voodoo-vodou/.

LaBorde, Lauren. "A Real Vodou Priestess on Cleansing Your Home of Evil Spirits and Negative Energy." Curbed New Orleans, 28 Oct. 2015, nola.curbed.com/2015/10/28/9906214/sallie-ann-glassman-home-cleanse-tips-voodoo.

Nana, Dr. "13 VOODOO SPELLS THAT ARE VERY POWERFUL and EFFECTIVE." Easy Spells, 9 Feb. 2020, lovespell.tips/13-vooodoo-spells-that-are-powerful-effective/.

Outpost, The. "Haitian Vodou: Summoning the Spirits | WilderUtopia.com." Www.wilderutopia.com, 30 Apr. 2013, www.wilderutopia.com/traditions/haitian-vodou-summoning-the-spirits/.

Refugiatei, Who made this site Design and Development Amy Marie Adams Arta. "James Duvalier." Jamesduvalier.com, jamesduvalier.com/history-beliefs-traditions-voodoo-part-haitian-vodou/

"Rituals, Traditions and Celebrations in Haiti." Usatoday.com, 2012, traveltips.usatoday.com/rituals-traditions-celebrations-haiti-103989.html.

"The Loa: Voodoo Spirits and How to Approach Them (for Witches)." Otherworldly Oracle, 18 Sept. 2019, otherworldlyoracle.com/loa-voodoo-spirits/.

The Voodoo Pantheon - Pagan. www.bellaonline.com/articles/art302082.asp.

Universe, Voodoo. "Creating Ancestor Altars in Santeria, Vodou, and Voodoo." Voodoo Universe, 23 Mar. 2014, www.patheos.com/blogs/voodoouniverse/2014/03/creating-ancestor-altars-in-santeria-vodou-and-voodoo/.

"Veve." Www.symbols.com, www.symbols.com/group/72/Veve.

"Voodoo - ReligionFacts." Religionfacts.com, religionfacts.com/voodoo.

"Voodoo - Rituals, World, Burial, Body, Life, Beliefs, Time, Person, Human." Deathreference.com, 2014, http://www.deathreference.com/Vi-Z/Voodoo.html.

"Voodoo Dolls." The Evil Wiki, evil.fandom.com/wiki/Voodoo_Dolls.

"Voodooria - an Authentic Voodoo Spell Casting Service." Voodooria, www.voodooria.com/.

"What Is the Doll?" Www.brown.edu, https://www.brown.edu/Departments/Joukowsky_Institute/courses/13things/7393.html

"11 Quick Cleansing Spells [for Your Spirit, House & Loved Ones]." Magickalspot.com, 2019,

magickalspot.com/cleansing-spells/.

"Augury Bird Divination: History & How to Read Bird Flight Patterns." Otherworldly Oracle, 2 May 2019,

otherworldlyoracle.com/augury-bird-divination-bird-flight-patterns/.

Candle Spells - Hoodoo Candle Rootwork | Conjure - Hoodoo - Witchcraft - Folk Magic. 22 July 2016,

www.southernfolkmagic.com/candle-spells/.

"Cleromancy - Throwing the Bones." The Bee Witch, http://www.mamabeewitch.com/mamabeesblog/throwing-the-bones.

Coles, Donyae. "Everyday Hoodoo: Washes, Mojo Bags, and Simple Charms." Spiral Nature Magazine, 30 July 2018, www.spiralnature.com/magick/hoodoo-washes-mojo-bags-charms/.

---. "Four Hoodoo Rituals for the Full Moon and Beyond." Wear Your Voice, 3 Nov. 2017,

wearyourvoicemag.com/use-full-moon-anchor-hoodoo-rituals/.

Conjure, Doc. "The Demoniacal: The Hoodoo Truth: The Christianity of Hoodoo." The Demoniacal, 7 Jan. 2012,

thedemoniacal.blogspot.com/2012/01/hoodoo-truth-christianity-of-hoodoo.html.

"ConjureDoctor.com - Home of Dr. E. Hoodoo Products and Magical Services, Get What You Want!" Conjuredoctor.com, conjuredoctor.com/index.php.

Damian, Angel. "AMAZING: 7 Surefire Rituals to Bring Money Your Way." Themagichoroscope.com, 26 Nov. 2020, themagichoroscope.com/zodiac/money-spells.

"Dream Divination * Wicca-Spirituality.com." https://www.wicca-spirituality.com/, https://www.wicca-spirituality.com/dream-divination.html.

"Dream Divination Ritual." The Digital Ambler, 14 June 2019, digitalambler.com/rituals/dream-divination-ritual/.

Eirecrescent. "A Natural Witch- Grimoire of Life and Practice: How to Make Talismans and Amulets." A Natural Witch- Grimoire of Life and Practice, 23 May 2013, naturalwitchlife.blogspot.com/2013/05/how-to-make-talismans-and-amulets.html.

"9 Staples of Every Soul Food Menu." Flavors Soul Food, 15 May 2017, www.flavorssoulfood.com/9-staples-every-soul-food-menu/

"Full Moon Astrology." Carolina Conjure, https://www.carolinaconjure.com/full-moon-astrology.html.

"Herbal Roots 101: How to Prepare and Use Roots for Wellness." Herbal Academy, 27 Nov. 2018,

theherbalacademy.com/herbal-roots-101/.

Hollywood, John. "5 Money Spells, Rituals, and Chants to Attract Wealth." Exemplore - Paranormal, exemplore.com/wicca-witchcraft/moneyspells.

Hoodoo and Rootwork Roots – Black Magic Witch. blackmagicwitch.com/magic-herb-glossary/hoodoo-and-rootwork-roots/

"Hoodoo Candle Magic." Hoodoo Magic Spells, 18 Aug. 2020, hoodoomagicspells.com/hoodoo-candle-magic/.

"Hoodoo Curios and Supplies - Dr. E. Products." Conjuredoctor.com, conjuredoctor.com/index.php?main_page=index&cPath=9.

Hoodoo Herbs - HoodooWitch. www.hoodoowitch.net/category/hoodoo-herbs/.

"Hoodoo, Rootwork, and Folk Magic: Olde Tales of the South." Otherworldly Oracle, 5 June 2018,

otherworldlyoracle.com/old-south-hoodoo-rootwork-folk-magic/

"Hoodoo Spells | EZ Spells." Www.ezspells.com, 29 June 2020, www.ezspells.com/hoodoo-spells/

Hoodoo Style Recipes - Black Witch Coven. blackwitchcoven.com/black-magick-spell-grimore/recipes-for-oils-incense/hoodoo-style-recipes/.

"How to Perform a House Cleansing in the Hoodoo Rootwork Tradition." Impact Shamanism, https://www.impactshamanism.com/blog/2019/1/18/how-to-perform-a-house-cleansing-in-the-hoodoo-rootwork-tradition

"Introduction to Hoodoo." Carolina Conjure, 2011, https://www.carolinaconjure.com/introduction-to-hoodoo.html.

"Lust Spells and Sex Magic." Wishbonix, 22 Sept. 2019, www.wishbonix.com/lust-spells/.

moodymoons. "The Ancient Art of Bone Reading for Beginners." Moody Moons, 29 Mar. 2019,

www.moodymoons.com/2019/03/29/the-ancient-art-of-bone-reading/.

"Recipes - Page 2." Hoodoo-Conjure.com, www.blog.hoodoo-conjure.com/category/recipes/page/2/.

Recipes: How to Prepare Different Hoodoo Powders - HoodooWitch. www.hoodoowitch.net/recipes-how-to-prepare-different-hoodoo-powders/

Sixth and Seventh Books of Moses - Occult World. occult-world.com/sixth-seventh-books-moses/.

"STEP-BY-STEP GUIDE on HOW to USE LOVE SPELLS." Www.hw-Group.com, www.hw-group.com/newsletter/list/how-to-use-love-spells.html.

"The Mojo." Carolina Conjure, https://www.carolinaconjure.com/the-mojo.html.

Universe, Voodoo. "Hoodoo House Blessing 101." Voodoo Universe, 14 Nov. 2017,

www.patheos.com/blogs/voodoouniverse/2017/11/hoodoo-house-blessing-101/.